D1080399

THE

Pudding Club

BOOK

If you would like to join The Pudding Club, or would like to know where you can attend one of its meetings, write to:

Keith and Jean Turner
The Pudding Club
The Croft
Mickleton
Chipping Campden
Glos. GL55 6RX

THE
Pudding Club
BOOK

Keith and Jean Turner

WITH

Annette Balfour Lynn

FOREWORD

BY

Chris Kelly

HEADLINE

First published in 1997 by HEADLINE BOOK PUBLISHING

10 9 8 7 6 5 4 3

BRITISH LIBRARY CATALOGUING IN PUBLICATION DATA
Turner, Keith
    The Pudding Club book
    1. Cookery (Puddings) 2. Puddings – Great Britain
    I. Title II. Turner, Joan
    641.8'64

ISBN 0 7472 2049 2

Edited by Susan Fleming
Designed by Peter Ward
Typeset by Letterpart Limited, Reigate, Surrey RH2 7BG
Printed and bound in Great Britain by Butler and Tanner Ltd

HEADLINE BOOK PUBLISHING
A division of Hodder Headline PLC
338 Euston Road
London NW1 3BH

CONTENTS

FOREWORD

PUDDING IS ONE of the loveliest words in the language. It's warm, plump and comforting. It's the feel-good factor in seven letters. In an uncertain world it's sweet and substantial. It speaks of reassurance and tradition. It's the fondest of all our food memories, and we can't talk about it without smiling.

In pudding, otherwise rational men and women find a common bond. You only have to mention spotted dick or jam roly-poly to trigger recollections from even the hardest heart. My first roly-polys were made by a homely cook called Mrs Egerton, who used to come and help my busy mother. She was the shape cooks ought to be; not tall and thin, like Marco Pierre White, but short and round. I can see her now, putting the great suety roll to bed in muslin, and I can taste the oozing jam, and smell the rich promise of seconds. See what I mean? Just to hear the word is to be instantly transported across the years.

So when I was invited to join The Pudding Club and celebrate our national treasure, I was delighted. We made a film of the visit for BBC2's Food and Drink programme. Who, I wondered, would turn up? Would we be a rather sad bunch of arrested adolescents, seeking comfort in custard? Would we be pudding bores, who could talk of nothing but the relative merits of Sussex pond pudding and ginger sponge? Would we all be immensely fat, indulging our sweet tooth until we could barely stand?

I was relieved to discover that we were none of these things. We were a cosmopolitan group who'd all come for the faintly ridiculous, nostalgic, fun of it. One couple had travelled all the way from Venezuela. True, they were taking in a couple of other big events on their trip, but The Pudding Club was unquestionably top of their must-do list. Jean and Keith, who invented the club and hosted the evening, had a genius for hospitality. Within minutes we all felt we'd known each other for half a lifetime.

The formula was simple. After a couple of drinks we sat down to a light main course and then got stuck in to the *pièces de résistance*. No fewer than seven heavenly puddings were paraded before us, amid fanfares and laughter. When we'd had our fill of them, we voted on the best, which was duly crowned and acclaimed. No-one took it seriously. I doubt if, half an hour later, anyone remembered which had won. But for three or four hours we were all bound by our enthusiasm for something wonderful and unchanging; something uncomplicated and unpretentious; something childish and yet enduring.

Earnest nutritionists will tell you puddings are bad for you. Emaciated diners in restaurants will shun desserts as though they were Satan's work. Well, to hell with all that. Puddings are glorious and life-enhancing. As long as you eat a pretty balanced diet you have absolutely nothing to fear. It's high time we pudding lovers made a stand. Bring back the great British pudding, I say. Let's see that evocative litany of menus both public and private. Let's revel in one of our greatest gastronomic assets. Let's join The Pudding Club – and live!

CHRIS KELLY

INTRODUCTION
TO THE
Pudding Club

LITTLE DID WE think, back in 1985, when we started The Pudding Club, that it would still be going strong over ten years later, and that we would write a book. We are very pleased, therefore, to present this collection of recipes which we hope will delight pudding-lovers of all ages. We still have cause to wonder what it is about The Pudding Club that attracts the attention, the passion even, of so many people. Mention 'The Pudding Club' and you get the sort of arm-clutching response that is usually reserved for the unexpected discovery of a long-lost friend or relative, and then follows an excited exchange about wonderful pudding experiences or how Auntie Mabel's bread pudding, even three days cold, had been the psychological anchor of our tender years.

As its founders, we wish we could say that The Pudding Club's growth and popularity were the result of careful planning on our part. Far from it. Actually, we started it almost as a joke, so a big debt of thanks is due to those who in its early days took it more seriously than we did. The particular hero amongst them was the gentleman who overheard our conversation in a pub in Malvern, when we got excited – over-excited probably – about puds we had known and loved, and resolved to organise an evening devoted to traditional puds. As we waxed ever more lyrical a bystander joined in, demanding to know more, and vowing that he would be there, no matter the distance or the difficulties in the way. He it was who got us started, because at his insistence, we fixed a date there and then, and the PC was launched.

Amongst other heroes and heroines are the hundreds of people who have supplied us with recipes over the years. We are sorry that it has not been possible to give them personal acknowledgements in this book, partly because many recipes have come to us from several different sources, and partly because many are very similar to other recipes of a different name. Safer to list no contributors than offend those who would have to be omitted, we thought. A sincere word of sympathy is due also to those who have sent us recipes which have not found their place in this book. Would that space could allow more!

There's also the problem of having to exclude some recipes that, while they are delicious creations in their own right, are not what most people would think of as puddings. Over the years we have learned that to try to define a pudding is not easy and carries the risk of excluding someone's treasured offering – rather like trying to tell a parent that their child isn't welcome at the party. For most pudding-lovers, the bench-marks of a true pud are that it will be a) hot and b) substantial. Further, c) it will probably have been cooked for a long time and d) – if there's still doubt – how comfortable is it with custard as a companion?

Ah, custard! Now there's a topic to excite the pudding-lover. When we started The Pudding Club, we took the purist approach and served the classic, straight-from-the-hen egg custard or crème anglaise. Club members quickly made it clear that this was not the accompaniment they were expecting for the traditional pud. What was needed was instant custard, they insisted, and not any old product would do. It must be Bird's Custard, they said. Over the years The Pudding Club has paid frequent homage to Alfred Bird by consuming, literally, hundreds of gallons of his worthy creation. We have even researched just the right degree of lumpiness to satisfy the insistent memories of Club members, which is to let the hot custard stand for just long enough to form a skin on the top and then stir it in.

Just as custard is nostalgic stuff, we came to acknowledge that nostalgia is an important element in all Pudding Club activities. A psychologist would no doubt tell us that each mouthful (psychologists are strong on mouthfuls) goes to the depth of our psyche, as much as into our stomach, as we reconnect with the caring warmth we knew, or wished we had known, when we were children. Not that such introspection would ever be voiced at Pudding Club meetings, with their atmosphere of 'the zestful spirit of yesteryear', as someone nicely put it.

The party atmosphere is another element in the ongoing success of The Pudding Club. Whoops! We nearly said 'essential ingredient', and some of our pudding-loving friends would have baulked at that. Our appetite for such figurative language is not to everyone's taste, they tell us, and plead for plainer fare, for words that don't carry the flavour of another meaning, which are not spiced with a pinch of pun or a slice of double-entendre. Undeterred, we point out that, after all, this is The Pudding Club, which is a pregnant phrase by any standards. (We were caught out by this on one occasion – hoist with our own petard indeed – see page 59.)

Another happy contributor to our success is the Club's philosophy of 'A little of what you fancy does you good'. We have discovered that this provides a welcome antidote to the modern-day preoccupation with 'healthy eating'. Nothing wrong with that, of course, but it does tend to engender either anxiety or guilt, or both, and seems to overlook one's state of mind as a factor – we would say *the* factor – in what constitutes healthy eating. There's a deep pleasure for anyone in sharing what they enjoy, and The Pudding Club has been fortunate to tap into that pleasure, which transforms the dining-out experience into a party with a lot of new friends. Thanks are due to those who have helped create the party atmosphere – those who have cheered or jeered at their host's awful jokes, who have interrupted his long-windedness, and generally harassed and heckled him with the greatest good humour.

A particular word of thanks and appreciation is due to Peter Henderson and Simon Coombe, who succeeded us at The Three Ways House Hotel in Mickleton, and who have been willing for it to take on the role of 'Home of The Pudding Club' and have hosted PC meetings there so graciously and skilfully. The hotel staff has earned the thanks of thousands of pudding-lovers for producing and serving high-quality puddings in great quantities, year in, year out. A rough calculation multiplies 65 pudding lovers on 220 occasions by an average of 5 helpings each and arrives at 70,000 portions of pud, accompanied by 400 gallons of custard. And still counting, as The Pudding Club continues to expand.

Expansion is taking place in two ways. Firstly, hotels and restaurants in other parts of the country which can meet The PC's high standards of quality and enthusiasm are being licensed to hold their own PC meetings. Secondly, we are creating a roll of PC members and making an individual's membership of The Pudding Club mean something in practical terms. (In the Club's earlier days, our answer to those who asked how they could join was to say that membership was automatic for any pudding-lover. Some were disappointed and have pressed us to make it a real association of like-minded folk.) So it is now possible for pudding-lovers to pay an annual subscription and thereby become members of The Pudding Club, receiving our twice-yearly *Feeder's Digest* of recipes and pudding venues, and getting a member's discount on various Pudding Club products, such as ties and aprons, and on admission to Pudding Club events (see page 2). This will also mean that pudding-lovers even in far-flung places can now admit their passion and play their part in our campaign even if they can't get to a Pudding Club meeting. We have been delighted to receive letters from pudding-lovers in places as far apart as the USA and South Africa, Canada and New Zealand.

INTRODUCTION 11

All this is evidence, if it were needed, that The Pudding Club is thriving. We admit to being surprised as well as gratified, considering that the original purpose of the Club – to ensure the survival of the species – has been achieved. In 1985 they were under threat, but now there are really good examples of tradition- al puds to be found in pubs and restaurants up and down the land; a major supermarket chain also sold a number of our puddings for some time. We express thanks and appreciation for the ready support for our cause from the press, radio and television. We particularly remember one local radio station where the fluency of the presenter became seriously obstructed by a too-hasty ingestion of syrup sponge. . . We wonder if they have yet managed to remove all the custard from his microphone.

And now what? Whither The Pudding Club as the twenty- first century beckons? Lay down our spoons and rest on our laurels? We think not. Already in this book there is a recipe for a new pudding – perhaps the first of many – to be called Millennium Pudding, as the next chapter in the story of The Pudding Club begins to unfold. And at last we may get round to a couple of projects dear to the hearts of some pudding-lovers, savoury puddings and milk puddings.

Our special thanks and appreciation to Annette Balfour Lynn, the instigator and researcher of this work, who kept bright the vision of a Pudding Club recipe book, through times when she was the only one who was confident that one day it would get into print, and through all the painstaking work of studying the hundreds of recipes that came her way. Thanks too to Mary Stokes, until lately chef at The Three Ways House Hotel, and other helpers who tested recipes to give them a final check before they went into the book. Finally, our thanks to the thousands of people who have come to meetings of The Pudding Club, even in the worst of winter weather, and to whom this book is gratefully dedicated.

KEITH AND JEAN TURNER

BASIC PUDDING INGREDIENTS

Puddings can be made from the simplest combination of basic standard items that most cooks have in the store-cupboard. Fresh eggs, milk, butter or margarine, bread and breadcrumbs, flour and sugar are the main ingredients, plus shredded suet. We recommend stocking up on them so that they can be combined for a variety of puddings without resorting to an extra shopping trip. However, that said, with the addition of a less usual ingredient or two, or with some fruit in season or tinned fruit, you have the capacity to make something really special. Nothing is more disappointing when the creative urge is upon you than to discover you are short of a vital ingredient. So we include a comprehensive list which should enable you to make the majority of our recipes at the drop of a hat.

EGGS AND MILK

Use medium eggs, free-range if possible, and whole milk.

FATS

Either butter or margarine can be used; margarine is somewhat lighter, although butter gives a better flavour. Use salted butter unless otherwise specified, and always add a pinch of salt when cooking with suet.

Suet gives a light, firm and rich texture to puddings and

pastry, and has no overpowering flavour, as it is a pure clarified fat. Once cooks would have had to clean and shred it at home, but ready shredded beef and vegetarian suet are now available in packets.

MARGARINE	SHREDDED (BEEF OR
SALTED BUTTER	VEGETARIAN) SUET
SUNFLOWER OIL	

BREAD AND BREADCRUMBS

Fresh white or wholemeal bread is used in some recipes. Breadcrumbs should always be used fresh (not dried), and should be white unless otherwise specified. Day-old bread is best for breadcrumbs. Remove the crusts, cut the bread into cubes, and chop in a food processor until fine. Make a larger quantity than needed, and store in a plastic bag in the freezer.

FLOURS, CEREALS AND RAISING AGENTS

PLAIN FLOUR	ROLLED OATS
SELF-RAISING FLOUR (WHITE	GROUND RICE
AND WHOLEMEAL)	SAGO
WHOLEMEAL FLOUR	BAKING POWDER
CORNFLOUR	BICARBONATE OF SODA

SWEETENERS

Nowadays granulated sugar is fine enough to use in most of the recipes, unless caster is specified. We also use demerara sugar and soft brown sugar, light or dark (or muscovado), depending on the colour or flavour desired.

Golden syrup replaces the black treacle mentioned in older recipes; add a tablespoon of black treacle (or molasses) to recipes for a darker, richer pudding.

GRANULATED SUGAR	GOLDEN SYRUP
CASTER SUGAR	BLACK TREACLE OR MOLASSES
DEMERARA SUGAR	HONEY
SOFT BROWN SUGAR	

DRIED FRUITS

These form the heart of a majority of traditional puddings. Buy the best you can get.

RAISINS	DATES
SULTANAS	FIGS
CURRANTS	PRUNES
MIXED DRIED FRUIT	GLACÉ CHERRIES
CANDIED CITRUS PEEL	APRICOTS

PRESERVES

Try to use home-made jams if possible, otherwise buy the best you can get.

JAMS (APRICOT, RASPBERRY, PLUM, DAMSON AND STRAWBERRY)	LEMON CURD
	PRESERVED STEM GINGER IN SYRUP
MARMALADE	CRYSTALLISED GINGER

NUTS

Buy nuts in the shell, or whole in packets, but don't keep too long, they do not last well.

ALMONDS, BLANCHED, SPLIT AND GROUND	HAZELNUTS
	DESICCATED COCONUT
WALNUTS	

FLAVOURINGS

ALMOND ESSENCE	GOOD PLAIN COOKING
VANILLA ESSENCE	CHOCOLATE
COCOA POWDER	CHOCOLATE CHIPS
CAMP COFFEE ESSENCE	

SPICES

As with nuts, ground spices do not keep their flavour for all that long. Keep in the dark, and replace frequently.

MIXED SPICE OR GROUND ALLSPICE	GROUND GINGER
	GROUND NUTMEG
CLOVES, WHOLE AND GROUND	
CINNAMON, WHOLE AND POWDERED	

PUDDING TECHNIQUES AND EQUIPMENT

'DEDICATED PEOPLE doing things in little clouds of steam, a mystery that needs probing,' enthused an American visitor to The Pudding Club. If there is a secret to steaming puddings, it is never to let the pan boil dry. To do that produces a disgusting smell, and spoils the pudding. A gentle rolling boil is best, because puddings that go off the boil can become heavy. Particularly recommended are the old-fashioned steamer pans that fit one on top of the other, enabling two or more puddings to be cooked at the same time (one to eat and one to freeze). The pudding sits in a perforated pan over another pan holding boiling water, under a tight-fitting lid. Steamers like this can often be found secondhand in boot fairs or jumble sales, and can of course be bought new from most kitchen shops and department stores. A portable kitchen timer or alarm clock set for every 30 minutes or so is a useful reminder to top up the water. Electric steamers have a built-in timer, and are programmed like kettles to switch off when they run dry.

However, a large saucepan with a tight lid is perfectly adequate. Here the pudding basin is actually in the boiling water and so the base of the basin needs to be kept off the base of the pan. To do this, make a trivet of metal knives or forks placed cross-wise at the bottom of the pan, or place a saucer or soup plate upside down with the pudding basin on top. Pour in boiling water to come halfway up the sides of the pudding basin.

Traditional ceramic pudding basins with a rim on the outside can still be found, but Pyrex, aluminium, enamel, plastic and foil pudding basins can all be used very satisfactorily. Always make sure the basin is large enough. Puddings can rise by about one-third, and if the basin is too small, the pudding can leak out, or push off the lid. Make sure the lid fits well.

To cover puddings securely in the old-fashioned way, first of all top with a circle of greaseproof paper, making a pleat to allow for the pudding to expand. Tie it tightly on with string under the rim, then add a circle of foil, also with a pleat, and tie again with string. Or use a pudding cloth instead of foil. Plastic basins need only a circle of greaseproof paper on top, plus the lid. Be sure, though, to fill them only two-thirds full to allow for expansion.

Make sure the basin is well greased with butter (or margarine) before filling with mixture. It helps to line the bottom with a small circle of greaseproof paper to enable the pudding to come out in one piece.

Leave the pudding to cool slightly before attempting to turn it out, by running a long thin-bladed knife around between basin and pudding. Try to do this in the privacy of the kitchen! If the pudding should break or fail to come out in one piece, disaster can be averted by simply reversing the pudding back into the basin, wrapping a large white napkin round it and serving it from the bowl, as they often do in restaurants.

Some puddings are traditionally boiled in cloths. Keep a supply of cloths approximately 15 in (38 cm) square: make them from old sheets or pillow cases, and keep them rolled up around sticks of cinnamon. A pudding cloth should naturally be very clean, and should be scalded (pour boiling water over it) before use. Dredge one side with flour. If for a round or bag pudding, put the cloth in a basin or bowl, floured side up. Add the pudding mixture and tie the cloth loosely at the top before lifting and lowering into the boiling water in a large pan. If the pudding cloth is large enough, the four corners can be lifted and tied together crossways

THE PUDDING CLUB BOOK

in pairs, which enables a wooden spoon to be inserted under the knots for lifting the pudding in and out, avoiding the steam. The mesh bags containing fruit from supermarkets (even the plastic ones) can also be used for this purpose. Put the pudding basin in the bag and tie the top in a knot; you can use this to lift the pudding out. A cylindrical pudding like roly-poly should be wrapped in cloth (loosely to allow for expansion), and then boiled in a suitable pan.

Move a cloth or bag pudding a few times during the boiling, as this prevents it sticking to the bottom of the pan. As with steaming, make sure the water is topped up as necessary.

Puddings can also be 'steamed' successfully in pressure cookers and microwave ovens, but follow the manufacturer's instructions carefully. Reheating in a microwave oven takes about 5 minutes for a large pudding, 1 minute for a slice.

A number of the puddings here are baked, and for this you need a selection of pie and baking dishes and loaf tins of varying sizes. You might be able to get hold of cylindrical tins which are used in commercial kitchens to make things like spotted dick. Most of the dishes should have deep sides, as many puddings rise more than you might expect, and many, particularly some fruit ones, make a lot of juice.

CHAPTER ONE

Winter Warmers

HERE WE LIST those puddings guaranteed to banish the blues, both physical and psychological, on even the coldest day.

We are reminded of just such a winter's night when the faithful had braved driving snow to attend a meeting of The Pudding Club. All went well until just before the Parade of the Puds when Keith, the Host for the evening, was informed by frantic whispering that there had been a disaster in the kitchen, and that the evening's entire custard production – 3 gallons of the stuff – had fallen to the floor, beyond recovery. Worse than that, until the morning delivery, there would not be enough milk to make more. Rejecting cowardly thoughts of serving cream or ice cream, our hero donned his wellies and set forth in the blizzard to visit the hotel's neighbour, a dairy farmer. In ten minutes he was back with two buckets of milk and the situation was retrieved, as was The Pudding Club's reputation for always providing 'lashings of custard'.

The end of the story lay with one of the guests who, ignorant of the drama behind the scenes, congratulated the Host on his thoughtfulness in having arranged such a useful and necessary pause between the main course and the puds. . .

Apple and Date Pudding

This is a good basic recipe, a robust suet pudding crust surrounding a tempting apple and date filling.

 Serves 4-6

6 OZ (180G) PLAIN FLOUR	1 LB (480G) COOKING APPLES,
A PINCH OF SALT	PEELED, CORED AND SLICED
1 TEASPOON BAKING POWDER	3 OZ (90G) STONED DATES, CHOPPED
2½ OZ (75G) SHREDDED SUET	A LITTLE SUGAR
COLD WATER TO MIX	JUICE OF ½ LEMON

Sieve the flour, salt and baking powder together, then add the suet and enough cold water to make a stiff dough. Roll out and line a greased 2 pint (1.1 litre) pudding basin, leaving enough dough for a lid. Fill with layers of sliced apples and chopped dates sprinkled with sugar and lemon juice, then top with the remaining dough. Wet the edges and press together. Cover securely and steam for 2-2½ hours. Turn out and serve with custard.

Winter Pudding

When wintry winds howl outside, keep the cold away with this hearty fruit pudding.

 Serves 4-6

3 OZ (90G) SELF-RAISING FLOUR	2 OZ (60G) SOFT BROWN SUGAR
A PINCH OF SALT	2 OZ (60G) SULTANAS
½ TEASPOON MIXED SPICE	2 OZ (60G) CURRANTS
3 OZ (90G) WHOLEMEAL BREADCRUMBS	2 OZ (60G) RAISINS
	FINELY GRATED RIND OF ½ LEMON
3 OZ (90G) SHREDDED SUET	MILK TO MIX

Sift the flour, salt and spice together. Stir in the breadcrumbs, suet, sugar, mixed dried fruit, and lemon rind and mix well. Stir in enough milk to make a soft dropping consistency. Spoon into a greased 2 pint (1.1 litre) pudding basin and cover securely. Steam for 2-2½ hours. Turn out and serve with custard.

Ginger Syrup Sponge

A moist ginger pudding with a soft syrup topping. Substituting a tablespoon of black treacle for an ounce (30g) of sugar gives it a good brown colour.

 Serves 4-6

2 TABLESPOONS GOLDEN SYRUP	6 OZ (180G) SELF-RAISING FLOUR
4 OZ (120G) MARGARINE	1 TEASPOON GROUND GINGER
3 OZ (90G) SOFT BROWN SUGAR	3 TABLESPOONS MILK
1 EGG, BEATEN	

Grease a 2 pint (1.1 litre) pudding basin and put the golden syrup in the bottom. Cream the margarine and sugar together, add the beaten egg and mix well. Sieve the flour and ginger together and fold into the mixture. Add the milk to form a dropping consistency. Spoon the mixture on top of the syrup. Cover securely and steam for 1½ hours. Serve with custard and warmed syrup.

Admiral's Pudding

This simple and robust pudding is made from a traditional ship's recipe, an eagerly awaited weekly treat for the sailors on a long sea trip.

 Serves 4-6

8 OZ (240G) SELF-RAISING FLOUR	½ TEASPOON MIXED SPICE
A PINCH OF SALT	1 TABLESPOON GOLDEN SYRUP
4 OZ (120G) SHREDDED SUET	1 EGG, BEATEN
6 OZ (180G) MIXED DRIED FRUIT	MILK TO MIX

Mix all the dry ingredients together, then add the syrup, beaten egg and enough milk to mix to a dropping consistency. Pour into a greased 2 pint (1.1 litre) pudding basin. Cover securely and steam for 2½-3 hours. Turn out and serve with custard.

Grandma's Chocolate Pudding

The use of cocoa powder makes for a strong chocolate flavour. Serve with custard, a vanilla-flavoured white sauce or a chocolate sauce.

 Serves 4-6

3 OZ (90G) MARGARINE OR BUTTER	5 OZ (150G) SELF-RAISING FLOUR
3 OZ (90G) SUGAR	1 HEAPED TABLESPOON COCOA
2 MEDIUM EGGS, BEATEN	POWDER

Mix or beat together the butter, sugar and eggs. Sieve together the flour and cocoa, and stir into the mixture. Pour into a well greased 2 pint (1.1 litre) pudding basin, cover securely and steam for 1½ hours. Turn out onto a warmed dish, and serve with one of the sauces suggested above (see pages 121-6).

Ginger Pudding

Until the Second World War, a centuries-old tradition continued in some taverns with customers helping themselves from a jar of ground ginger to spice their tankards of porter.

 Serves 4-6

8 OZ (240G) SELF-RAISING FLOUR	3 TABLESPOONS GOLDEN SYRUP
A PINCH OF SALT	1 TEASPOON BICARBONATE OF
1 TEASPOON GROUND GINGER	SODA MIXED WITH 3 FL OZ
3-4 OZ (90-120G) SHREDDED SUET	(100ML) TEPID WATER

Sieve the flour, salt and ginger together. Mix in the remaining ingredients, and turn into a greased 2 pint (1.1 litre) pudding basin. Cover securely and steam for 2½ hours. Turn out and serve with Syrup Sauce (see page 122).

Raisin Ginger Pudding

A recipe dating from before the First World War provides the opportunity to experiment with a topping – a few extra raisins perhaps, or some nuts. A little chopped preserved ginger in the mixture adds interest to the texture.

 Serves 4-6

4 OZ (120G) PLAIN FLOUR	1 TEASPOON GROUND ALLSPICE
½ TEASPOON BICARBONATE OF	3 OZ (90G) SHREDDED SUET
SODA	3 OZ (90G) RAISINS
A PINCH OF SALT	2 OZ (60G) GOLDEN SYRUP
4 OZ (120G) BREADCRUMBS	MILK TO MIX
1 TEASPOON GROUND GINGER	

Sift the flour, bicarbonate and salt together, then mix in all the remaining dry ingredients. Melt the syrup, add to the mixed dry ingredients and stir in enough milk to make a dropping consistency. Spoon into a greased 2 pint (1.1 litre) pudding basin, cover securely and steam for 3 hours. Turn out and serve with custard or Ginger Sauce (see page 124).

Orange Pudding

This loaf-shaped pudding is baked in the oven. You can serve it as a hot pudding with cream or custard, or slice it cold at tea-time.

 Serves 4-6

3 TABLESPOONS MARMALADE	FINELY GRATED RIND AND JUICE
2 SMALL ORANGES, SCRUBBED AND	OF 1 LEMON
THINLY SLICED	2 EGGS, BEATEN
3 OZ (90G) SELF-RAISING FLOUR	2 OZ (60G) BREADCRUMBS
½ TEASPOON POWDERED CINNAMON	3 OZ (90G) GLACÉ CHERRIES,
4 OZ (120G) BUTTER	CHOPPED
4 OZ (120G) CASTER SUGAR	3 OZ (90G) SULTANAS

Preheat the oven to 200°C/400°F/Gas 6.

Grease the base and sides of a 2 lb (960g) loaf tin (or a 2 pint/1.1 litre ovenproof pudding basin). Spread the base and sides with the marmalade, then line with the orange slices. Sift the flour and cinnamon together. Cream the butter, sugar and lemon rind together until fluffy. Gradually beat in the eggs and fold in the sifted flour and breadcrumbs. Finally, gently stir in the fruit and lemon juice and spoon into the prepared tin. Cover with foil and bake for 1½ hours, or until firm. Turn out and serve with cream or custard.

Four Fruit Pudding

A good hearty pudding containing dates, figs, prunes and mixed peel.

 ## Serves 4-6

4 OZ (120G) PLAIN FLOUR	1 OZ (30G) DRIED FIGS, CHOPPED
A PINCH OF SALT	1 OZ (30G) STONELESS PRUNES,
1½ LEVEL TEASPOONS BAKING	CHOPPED
POWDER	1 OZ (30G) MIXED PEEL, CHOPPED
4 OZ (120G) BREADCRUMBS	3 OZ (90G) SHREDDED SUET
3 OZ (90G) CASTER SUGAR	1 LARGE EGG, BEATEN
1 OZ (30G) STONED DATES,	4 FL OZ (125ML) MILK
CHOPPED	

Sift the flour, salt and baking powder into a mixing bowl, then add the remaining dry ingredients. Mix to a soft batter with the beaten egg and milk. Turn into a greased 2 pint (1.1 litre) pudding basin. Cover securely and steam for 2½-3 hours. Turn out and serve with custard.

 ## Tip

A good way of recycling leftover pudding is to cut it into slices, lay them in an ovenproof dish, and pour over a custard made from roughly ¾ pint (450ml) milk mixed with 2 beaten eggs and 2 oz (60g) sugar. Leave to soak until soft, then dab with butter and bake in a 200°C/400°F/Gas 6 oven until the custard has set, and the top is invitingly golden brown.

Caramel Pudding

This recipe from The Pudding Club archive is expressed only in cups, which makes it quick and easy. The larger the cup, the larger the pudding!

 Serves 4-6

1½ CUPS PLAIN FLOUR	I CUP RAISINS OR SULTANAS (OR
2 TEASPOONS BAKING POWDER	A MIXTURE OF BOTH)
I CUP MILK	

Sauce

2 CUPS BOILING WATER	I CUP BROWN SUGAR
I TABLESPOON BUTTER	

Preheat the oven to 180°C/350°F/Gas 4.

Sieve the flour and baking powder into a bowl, add the dried fruit and milk, and spread over the base of a greased 2 pint (1.1 litre) baking dish. Mix together the boiling water, butter and brown sugar and pour over the pudding. Bake for 30-40 minutes. A sponge pudding forms on top with a creamy caramel sauce underneath.

Sultana and Butterscotch Pudding

This is a more elaborate pudding, on the same lines as Caramel Pudding. Make sure the dish is deep enough to hold the pudding mixture and the sauce, as it is very liquid when going into the oven. Either butter or margarine can be used for the pudding, but the former gives a better flavour to the sauce.

 ## Serves 4-6

2½ OZ (75G) BUTTER OR MARGARINE	4 OZ (120G) SULTANAS (OR MIXED
5 OZ (150G) PLAIN FLOUR	DRIED FRUIT)
2 TEASPOONS BAKING POWDER	2¾ FL OZ (90ML) MILK
2 OZ (60G) SUGAR	I EGG, BEATEN

Sauce

4 OZ (120G) SOFT BROWN SUGAR	¾ PINT (450ML) BOILING WATER
1½ OZ (45G) BUTTER	JUICE OF ½ LEMON

Preheat the oven to 180°C/350°F/Gas 4.

Grease a 2 pint (1.1 litre) baking dish. Rub the margarine or butter into the flour until it is like fine crumbs, then add the baking powder, sugar and fruit. Mix to a dropping consistency with the milk and egg. Spread into the greased pie dish. Make the sauce by melting the sugar and butter in a saucepan. Add the boiling water and lemon juice. When mixed, pour gently over the pudding mixture. It looks very runny at this stage. Bake in the oven for 30-45 minutes. The pudding rises to a golden brown crumbly texture, with a delicious sauce underneath.

Winter Pear Pudding

This is a moist, dark and spicy baked Victorian pudding. Its topping of glistening red cherries in a wheel of pears gives it a festive air.

 Serves 6

3 PEARS PEELED, HALVED AND CORED	¼ PINT (150ML) MILK, LUKEWARM
A LITTLE MELTED BUTTER	1 LEVEL TEASPOON BICARBONATE OF SODA
3 LEVEL TABLESPOONS DEMERARA SUGAR	8 OZ (240G) PLAIN FLOUR
	A PINCH OF SALT
6 GLACÉ CHERRIES	1 LEVEL TEASPOON POWDERED
4 OZ (120G) LARD	CINNAMON
4 OZ (120G) GOLDEN SYRUP	1 LEVEL TEASPOON GROUND GINGER
4 OZ (120G) BLACK TREACLE	3 OZ (90G) SOFT BROWN SUGAR
1 EGG, BEATEN	

Preheat the oven to 180°C/350°F/Gas 4.

Line the base and sides of a deep 8 in (20cm) round cake tin with greaseproof paper, and brush over with melted butter. Sprinkle the base with the demerara sugar. Where the core has been removed from the pear, place a cherry. Put the pears cut side down on the sugar, radiating from the centre, narrow ends in. The pears may need trimming to fit.

Place the lard, syrup and treacle in a small pan over a low heat until the lard has melted. Stir together the beaten egg, milk and bicarbonate of soda. Sift the flour, salt, cinnamon and ginger into a mixing bowl and stir in the soft brown sugar. Make a well in the centre and pour in the melted lard mixture and the egg mixture. Stir together, and beat until smooth and glossy. Pour over the pears in the tin. Bake in the centre of the oven for 45 minutes to 1 hour, or until well risen and firm to the touch. Test with a skewer in the middle if in doubt. Turn the pudding out on to a warm plate, pears up, and peel away the paper. Serve everyone a piece of pear, with an accompanying custard or soured cream sauce.

Tip

This pudding can also be made in an 8 in (20cm) square tin. Use four pears cut in half, and arrange, face down, three halves on either side with two down the middle. In between the pears arrange walnut or Brazil nut halves – or use your imagination!

To make soured cream sauce, stir a small carton of plain yoghurt into a small carton of double cream, whipped.

Gingerbread Pudding

Ginger is one of those flavours you either like or you don't. With this pudding, even the doubtful ones can be won over by the addition of a butterscotch sauce.

 Serves 4-6

2 OZ (60G) PLAIN FLOUR	2 TEASPOONS GROUND GINGER
¼ TEASPOON BAKING POWDER	I EGG, BEATEN
6 OZ (180G) BREADCRUMBS	2 TABLESPOONS GOLDEN SYRUP
4 OZ (120G) SHREDDED SUET	

Sieve the flour and baking powder together, then mix in the bread-crumbs, suet and ginger. Add the beaten egg with the syrup. Mix thoroughly and put into a greased 2 pint (1.1 litre) pudding basin. Cover securely and steam for 3 hours. Turn out and serve with the Butterscotch Sauce on page 123.

Lemon and Ginger Pudding

Lemon and ginger make an ideal combination.

 Serves 4-6

3 TEASPOONS DEMERARA SUGAR	2 OZ (60G) BUTTER OR MARGARINE
I LEMON	I EGG, BEATEN
4 OZ (120G) SELF-RAISING FLOUR	2–3 TABLESPOONS MILK
1½ LEVEL TEASPOONS GROUND GINGER	2 OZ (60G) GOLDEN SYRUP

Grease a 2 pint (1.1 litre) pudding basin. Sprinkle a thick crust of brown sugar all over the inside of the basin. Finely grate the rind of the lemon, and then peel off the remaining peel and pith. Cut the lemon into thin slices and use these to line the base and sides of the basin. Sift the flour and ginger together, then rub in the butter or margarine until it is like fine crumbs. Add the egg and mix in with the lemon rind, milk and syrup. Pour gently into the lemon-lined basin, cover securely and steam for 2 hours. Turn out and serve with custard.

Tip

To remove pith from a lemon, use a very small sharp knife – or a swivel potato peeler is good.

Orange Pudding, decorated here with thin curls of
orange peel, can be served hot or cold.
See page 26.

 When baked, the golden brown sponge of Sultana and
Butterscotch Pudding sits on top of its own delicious sauce.
See page 29.

In Blackberry Exeter Pudding, a suet pastry
encloses an autumnal filling of blackberries and apples.
See page 45.

 A cooked Apple Charlotte looks like a buttery
brown loaf full of soft fragrant apples.
See page 51.

Carrot Pudding

A dark, rich, fruity pudding, with the unusual addition of potatoes. It is very important with this pudding to mix the ingredients together in the order given, adding just enough liquid to make a dropping consistency.

 Serves 4-6

2 OZ (60G) SELF-RAISING FLOUR	4 OZ (120G) MIXED DRIED FRUIT
2 OZ (60G) BREADCRUMBS	2 OZ (60G) RAW CARROT, PEELED
1 OZ (30G) SUGAR	AND GRATED
A PINCH OF SALT	2 OZ (60G) RAW POTATO, PEELED
½ TEASPOON MIXED SPICE	AND GRATED
2 OZ (60G) SHREDDED SUET	2 TEASPOONS BLACK TREACLE
2 OZ (60G) CANDIED PEEL,	A PINCH OF BICARBONATE OF SODA
CHOPPED	ORANGE JUICE TO MIX

Grease a 2½-3 pint (1.4-1.7 litre) pudding basin. After mixing the ingredients together, turn into the basin and cover securely. Steam for 2½-3 hours. Turn out on to a warmed plate and serve with custard.

Spicy Fruit Pudding

Add 2 tablespoons marmalade to the bottom of the basin for a soft orange topping when you turn it out.

 Serves 4-6

4 OZ (120G) SELF-RAISING FLOUR	¼ TEASPOON POWDERED CINNAMON
A PINCH OF SALT	¼ TEASPOON GROUND GINGER
½ TEASPOON BAKING POWDER	¼ TEASPOON MIXED SPICE
2 OZ (60G) BREADCRUMBS	2 OZ (60G) GOLDEN SYRUP
2 OZ (60G) SHREDDED SUET	I EGG, BEATEN
4 OZ (120G) SOFT BROWN SUGAR	MILK TO MIX
4 OZ (120G) MIXED DRIED FRUIT	

Sift the flour, salt and baking powder together, then add the remaining dry ingredients. Add the syrup, beaten egg and enough milk to make a dropping consistency. Spoon into a greased 2 pint (1.1 litre) pudding basin. Cover securely and steam for 2 hours. Turn out and serve with custard or Orange Sauce (see page 122).

Date and Lemon Pudding

A lemon-flavoured custard will complement this pudding filled with dates, mixed fruit and lemon.

 Serves 4-6

1 TABLESPOON LEMON CURD	FINELY GRATED RIND AND JUICE
3 OZ (90G) PLAIN FLOUR	OF 1 LEMON
½ TEASPOON SALT	4 FL OZ (125ML) MILK
1 TEASPOON BAKING POWDER	½ OZ (15G) SUGAR
3 OZ (90G) BREADCRUMBS	3 OZ (90G) SHREDDED SUET
10 OZ (300G) MIXED DRIED FRUIT	1 EGG, BEATEN
3 OZ (90G) STONED DATES, CHOPPED	

Place the lemon curd in the bottom of a greased 2 pint (1.1 litre) pudding basin. Sieve the flour, salt and baking powder into a large bowl. Stir in the remaining ingredients and mix well. Pour into the prepared pudding basin, cover securely and steam for 2 hours. Turn out the pudding and serve with Lemon Custard Sauce (see page 126).

Treacle Tart

Sweet and sticky enough to satisfy most people with a sweet tooth. Of the many treacle tart recipes, this is the one The Pudding Club prefers.

 Serves 4-6

Pastry

8 OZ (240G) PLAIN FLOUR	2 TABLESPOONS WATER
I PINCH OF SALT	BEATEN EGG TO GLAZE
5 OZ (150G) MARGARINE	

Filling

6 OZ (180G) GOLDEN SYRUP	FINELY GRATED RIND AND JUICE
2 OZ (60G) BREADCRUMBS	OF I LEMON OR ORANGE

Preheat the oven to 190°C/375°F/Gas 5.

Sift the flour and salt together, then rub in the margarine until the mixture resembles fine crumbs. Add the water, and mix to a firm dough. Turn out on to a floured board and let it rest for 20 minutes. Roll out and line an 8 in (20cm) pie plate with three-quarters of the pastry, keeping the rest in reserve for decoration.

Warm the syrup, mix with the crumbs, and spread in the pastry case. Pour over the lemon or orange juice and sprinkle with the rind. Roll out the extra pastry and cut into ½ in (1cm) wide strips. Arrange them over the filling in a criss-cross pattern to make a pretty lattice top. Brush with beaten egg. Bake for 30-40 minutes. Serve with whipped cream or custard.

Tip

To help measure the syrup when it needs warming for this pudding, weigh the saucepan and then add on the weight of the syrup needed. Spoon syrup into the saucepan until the weight required is reached.

Charlotte's Raisin Pudding

This delicious pudding looks a little unappetising in the making, but don't be put off. Sago is the ingredient that gives the unusual texture. A similar recipe using sago is Chiltern Hills Pudding, and the only difference between the two is 1 oz (30g) of suet.

 Serves 4-6

2 TABLESPOONS SAGO	1 EGG, BEATEN
2 OZ (60G) MARGARINE	½ TEASPOON BICARBONATE OF
4 OZ (120G) SUGAR	SODA, DISSOLVED IN A LITTLE
6 OZ (180G) BREADCRUMBS	MILK
3 OZ (90G) RAISINS	MILK TO MIX

Soak the sago overnight in water, then drain well. Cream the margarine and sugar together, then mix in the drained sago, the breadcrumbs, raisins, beaten egg, bicarbonate of soda and enough milk to make a pouring consistency. Pour into a greased 2 pint (1.1 litre) pudding basin, cover securely and steam for 3 hours. Turn out on to a warmed plate and serve with custard.

Grandma's Pudding

Despite what appears to be a large amount of carrots, this is a small but tasty pudding. Doubling the quantities makes it a good, light, family-sized Christmas pudding.

 Serves 4

2 LB (960G) CARROTS, PEELED AND GRATED	2 OZ (60G) BREADCRUMBS
4 OZ (120G) SELF-RAISING FLOUR	4 OZ (120G) SHREDDED SUET
A PINCH OF SALT	I TEASPOON GROUND NUTMEG
4 OZ (120G) SUGAR	4 OZ (120G) LARGE SULTANAS
	¼ PINT (150 ML) CIDER

Boil the carrots until soft, then strain and mash and leave to cool. Sift the flour and salt together, then mix in all the remaining ingredients. Add the carrots and mix well. Cover and leave in the fridge overnight to allow the flavours to mingle. Put into a greased 2 pint (1.1 litre) pudding basin, cover securely and steam for 2 hours. Turn out on to a warmed plate and serve with Rich White Sauce (see page 126).

Canary Pudding

Add 2 tablespoons of apricot jam or golden syrup to the pudding basin for an even sunnier-looking pudding.

 Serves 4-6

4 OZ (120G) BUTTER	FINELY GRATED RIND AND JUICE
4 OZ (120G) CASTER SUGAR	OF 1 LEMON
2 EGGS, BEATEN	1-2 TABLESPOONS MADEIRA OR
2 OZ (60G) SELF-RAISING FLOUR	SWEET SHERRY
2 OZ (60G) BREADCRUMBS	

Cream the butter and sugar together until light and fluffy. Add the eggs gradually, beating well. Fold the sieved flour into the mixture, then carefully stir in the crumbs and rind. Mix to a soft dropping consistency with the Madeira and lemon juice. Spoon into a well greased 2 pint (1.1 litre) pudding basin, cover securely and steam for 2½ hours. Serve with Lemon Sauce (see page 122) or custard.

Black Cap Pudding

 Use the same sponge mixture as Canary Pudding, putting either 3 tablespoons blackcurrant jam or a good sprinkling of dried currants in the basin before adding the mixture.

Oriental Ginger Pudding

This recipe for ginger pudding is slightly extravagant, using preserved ginger in syrup which adds interest to the texture.

 Serves 4-6

6 OZ (180G) SELF-RAISING FLOUR	1½ OZ (45G) PRESERVED STEM GINGER, DRAINED AND CHOPPED
A PINCH OF SALT	
1½ HEAPED TEASPOONS GROUND GINGER	3 TABLESPOONS GOLDEN SYRUP, WARMED
3 OZ (90G) SHREDDED SUET	1 EGG, BEATEN
1½ OZ (45G) SOFT BROWN SUGAR	

Sieve together the flour, salt and ground ginger. Mix with the suet, sugar and chopped stem ginger. Add the warmed syrup and the egg, and mix well. Transfer to a greased 2 pint (1.1 litre) pudding basin, cover securely and steam for 1½ hours. Turn out on to a warmed dish and serve with extra syrup and custard.

Guard's Pudding

This is a moist jammy pudding with a moist jammy topping.

 Serves 4-6

3 TABLESPOONS RASPBERRY OR STRAWBERRY JAM	2 EGGS, BEATEN
4 OZ (120G) BUTTER	A PINCH OF SALT
4 OZ (120G) SOFT BROWN SUGAR	½ TEASPOONS BICARBONATE OF SODA DISSOLVED IN 1 TABLESPOON WARM WATER
4 OZ (120G) BROWN BREADCRUMBS	

Grease a 2 pint (1.1 litre) pudding basin and put a large tablespoon of jam in the bottom. Cream the butter and sugar together until fluffy, then blend in the remaining jam. Add the breadcrumbs, beaten eggs, salt and bicarbonate of soda in water. Mix well and turn into the basin. Cover securely and steam for 2½ hours. Turn out and serve with custard.

Bread Pudding

Leftover bread, buns, crumpets and muffins can all be used in some way to make tasty bread puddings. This is The Pudding Club version of this well-known pudding.

 Serves 4-6

12 OZ (360G) BREAD, INCLUDING CRUSTS	2 TEASPOONS MIXED SPICE
	1 TABLESPOON GOLDEN SYRUP
3 OZ (90G) SHREDDED SUET	1 OZ (30G) DEMERARA SUGAR
2 OZ (60G) CASTER SUGAR	A LITTLE BUTTER
8 OZ (240G) MIXED DRIED FRUIT	

Preheat the oven to 190°C/375°F/Gas 5.

Cut the bread up roughly, put in a basin, and saturate with cold water. Leave to soften, then turn into a colander and squeeze out as much liquid as possible. Put the bread into a mixing bowl and beat with a fork until smooth. Add the suet, sugar, fruit, spice and syrup. When thoroughly mixed, turn into a greased ovenproof dish about 7 in (18cm) square. Smooth the surface, sprinkle with demerara sugar and a few dabs of butter, and bake for 1 hour. Serve hot with custard or cream. (It's also very good when cold.)

CHAPTER TWO

Seasonal Surprises

HERE WE HONOUR the wonderful variety of fruits that come in their season. Nowadays fruit preservation, refrigeration and freight-by-air make many fruits accessible all the year round, but there is still a special delight in meeting the real thing in a pudding, perhaps only a few hours after it was picked.

One of our favourite memories was the newcomer to The Pudding Club, attending his first meeting, and letting it be known that he didn't like puddings, that they were not part of his diet, and that he was present only as an escort to his wife. More than that, he asked the Host for the Evening if he might have cheese and biscuits instead of all those puddings. The effrontery of it! (The sort of shock-horror situation which would inspire an H.M. Bateman cartoon – The Man Who Asked For Cheese At The Pudding Club.)

Later in the evening when the Host had relented, and was about to serve the cheese and biscuits (covered discreetly by a cloth, of course), the gentleman in question was seen to be tucking into a large helping of pud. This was followed by another helping, and then another. At the end of the evening, the pudding-hater generously admitted that he had enjoyed himself very much. It was the rhubarb crumble that did it, he said. He hadn't had rhubarb for forty years and one taste had been enough to make him realise that his diet was in need of review. Not a word was said about cheese and biscuits. . .

Syrup and Apple Sponge Pudding

Like one or two others in this book, this might, from its ingredients, be judged as dull, but do not be deterred! Savour the simple sharp sweetness which endeared it to previous generations.

 Serves 4-6

8 OZ (240G) SELF-RAISING FLOUR	I EGG, BEATEN
3 OZ (90G) MARGARINE	MILK TO MIX
3 OZ (90G) SUGAR	3 TABLESPOONS GOLDEN SYRUP
FINELY GRATED RIND OF ½ LEMON	I LARGE COOKING APPLE, PEELED
½ TEASPOON POWDERED CINNAMON	AND CORED

Sieve the flour. Rub the margarine into the flour until the texture is like fine crumbs, then add the sugar, lemon rind and cinnamon. Mix with the egg and enough milk to make a soft dropping consistency. Grease a 3 pint (1.7 litre) pudding basin, spread the syrup at the base, and thinly slice the apple on top. Spoon in the pudding mixture, cover securely and steam for 1½ hours. Turn out and serve with custard, or syrup melted with a little lemon juice.

Rhubarb Hat

A good filling pudding for those chilly early spring days, making use of young pink rhubarb.

Serves 4-6

Suet pastry

8 OZ (240G) SELF-RAISING FLOUR	A PINCH OF SALT
4 OZ (120G) SHREDDED SUET	WATER TO MIX

Filling

1 LB (480G) FRESH RHUBARB, CHOPPED	2 OZ (60G) SHREDDED SUET
	4 OZ (120G) RUNNY HONEY
8 OZ (240G) BREADCRUMBS	1 TEASPOON GROUND GINGER

Mix the suet pastry ingredients together to form a fairly stiff dough. Divide the pastry into two-thirds and one-third. Use the larger piece to line a greased 2 pint (1.1 litre) pudding basin. Reserve the smaller piece for the lid.

For the filling, combine the breadcrumbs, suet, honey and ginger. Place half of the chopped rhubarb into the base of the lined basin. Cover with half of the suet and crumb mixture and top with rhubarb again. Cover with the remaining suet and crumb mixture. Roll out the remaining pastry and place on top of the pudding, wetting the edges to make it stick. Cover securely and steam for 2-3 hours. Turn out and serve with custard.

Blackberry Exeter Pudding

Follow the recipe for Rhubarb Hat, but substitute 8 oz (240g) blackberries, and 8 oz (240g) of chopped apple for the rhubarb. Other seasonal fruits and berries can also be used.

Apple and Walnut Pudding

A delicious moist baked pudding, equally good made with plums or prunes instead of apples. The original manuscript recipe in The Pudding Club archives describes this as an 'excellent healthy pudding'.

 Serves 4-6

1 LB (480G) COOKING APPLES, PEELED AND CORED	4 OZ (120G) SOFT BROWN SUGAR
2 OZ (60G) SHELLED WALNUTS	1 OZ (30G) BUTTER, MELTED
4 OZ (120G) STONED DATES	1 TABLESPOON HONEY
4 OZ (120G) WHOLEMEAL SELF-RAISING FLOUR	1 EGG, BEATEN

Preheat the oven to 200°C/400°F/Gas 6.

Chop the apples, walnuts and dates into small pieces. Sift the flour, then mix with all the remaining ingredients, including the fruit. Place in a greased 8 in (20cm) square baking dish or cake tin and bake for about half an hour. Serve warm with cream.

Plum and Almond Pudding

Home-made jam is always best. However, when using bought jam, make sure it is a good quality, as cheaper jam is sometimes a bit thick, and fails to soak into the mixture. The sponge mixture is a good basic one and lends itself very well to other combinations.

 Serves 4-6

4 OZ (120G) CASTER SUGAR	I TABLESPOON GROUND ALMONDS
4 OZ (120G) BUTTER OR	OR CHOPPED ALMONDS
MARGARINE	¼ TEASPOON ALMOND ESSENCE
2 EGGS, BEATEN	2 TABLESPOONS STEWED PLUMS
6 OZ (180G) SELF-RAISING FLOUR	OR PLUM JAM

Grease a 3 pint (1.7 litre) pudding basin. Cream the sugar and butter or margarine together until light and fluffy. Beat in the eggs, with a little sieved flour, then fold in the remaining flour and the almonds and almond essence. Place the jam or plums in the bottom of the basin and pour in the pudding mixture. Cover securely and steam for 1½-2 hours. Turn out and serve hot with custard.

Baked Apple Sponge

Make a simple pudding with just one apple and a light sponge mixture.

 Serves 4-6

4 OZ (120G) SELF-RAISING FLOUR	2 EGGS, BEATEN
4 OZ (120G) MARGARINE	I MEDIUM COOKING APPLE,
4 OZ (120G) DEMERARA SUGAR	PEELED, CORED AND CHOPPED

Preheat the oven to 190°C/375°F/Gas 5.

Sift the flour. Cream the margarine and sugar together, then slowly add the beaten eggs with a little flour. Fold in the remaining flour and the apple. Spoon into a greased 2 pint (1.1 litre) ovenproof dish and bake for 15 minutes, then reduce heat slightly to 180°C/350°F/Gas 4, and continue baking for another 20 minutes. Serve hot with custard or cream.

Rustic Pudding

Any juicy fruit will do for this bread and fruit pudding. Here greengage plums are used, but gooseberries and redcurrants would be a deliciously tart combination.

 Serves 4-6

ABOUT HALF A LARGE LOAF OF	2 LB (960G) GREENGAGES, STEWED
BREAD IN THIN SLICES, CRUSTS	BRIEFLY AND STONED
REMOVED	CASTER SUGAR TO TASTE
2 OZ (60G) BUTTER, SOFTENED	LEMON JUICE TO TASTE

Preheat the oven to 180°C/350°F/Gas 4.

Grease a deep 2 pint (1.1 litre) pie dish. Butter the bread thinly. Arrange most of the bread, plus the fruit and its juices, sugar and lemon juice in layers. Finish with a layer of bread, buttered side up, and sprinkled with sugar. Bake for 30-45 minutes. Serve with cream or custard.

Lemon Surprise Pudding

A light fluffy sponge pudding with a thick lemon sauce underneath.

 Serves 4-6

4 OZ (120G) BUTTER	4 EGGS, SEPARATED
6 OZ (180G) CASTER SUGAR	16 FL OZ (500ML) MILK
2 TABLESPOONS PLAIN FLOUR	
FINELY GRATED RIND AND JUICE	
OF 2 LARGE LEMONS	

Preheat the oven to 180°C/350°F/Gas 4.

Cream the softened butter and sugar together, then stir in the flour, grated rind and juice of the lemons, the egg yolks and milk. Fold in the well-beaten egg whites. Pour into a greased 2 pint (1.1 litre) pudding dish and bake for 30-45 minutes. Serve with single cream.

Pineapple Upside-down Pudding

You can use fresh pineapple for this pudding. Peel and core, then slice and poach gently for a few minutes in water with a little sugar.

 ### Serves 4-6

I X 220G TIN OF PINEAPPLE RINGS	2 OZ (60G) SUGAR
6-8 GLACÉ CHERRIES	2 OZ (60G) BUTTER
6-8 WALNUT HALVES	

Sponge

4 OZ (120G) BUTTER	2 EGGS, BEATEN
4 OZ (120G) CASTER SUGAR	5 OZ (150G) SELF-RAISING FLOUR
FINELY GRATED RIND AND JUICE	
OF I ORANGE	

Preheat the oven to 180°C/350°F/Gas 4.

Grease the sides of an 8 in (20cm) deep sandwich tin or a square tin (not one with a loose bottom). Drain the pineapple rings and keep the juice. Arrange the pineapple rings on the base of the tin and decorate in a pattern with cherries and nuts. Make the pineapple juice up to ¼ pint (150ml), and put in a pan with the sugar and butter. Heat to dissolve the sugar, stirring, then pour over the pineapple.

For the sponge, cream the butter, sugar and orange rind together and then add the beaten eggs. Fold in the sieved flour and the orange juice. Spoon the mixture over the fruit, and bake for 40-45 minutes. Leave for a few minutes before turning out, pineapple up. Serve with custard.

Autumn Pudding

A good pudding which combines sultanas, orange juice and an apple, but other autumn fruits, such as a pear or a quince, would make a good substitute for the apple.

 Serves 4-6

4 OZ (120G) SELF-RAISING FLOUR	I EGG, BEATEN
A PINCH OF SALT	4 OZ (120G) GOLDEN SYRUP
4 OZ (120G) BREADCRUMBS	JUICE AND FINELY GRATED RIND
4 OZ (120G) SHREDDED SUET	OF ½ ORANGE
4 OZ (120G) SULTANAS	I LARGE COOKING APPLE, PEELED,
3 OZ (90G) CASTER SUGAR	CORED AND CHOPPED OR GRATED

Sieve the flour and salt together and mix with all the dry ingredients. Blend the beaten egg with the golden syrup and orange rind and juice, then add to the mixture with the chopped or grated apple. Mix well and turn into a greased 2 pint (1.1 litre) pudding basin. Cover securely and steam for 3 hours. Turn out and serve with custard.

Apple Charlotte

There is a degree of culinary controversy over the name 'charlotte'. Some writers claim that it was named and created for George III's Queen. In fifteenth-century recipes the word 'charlet' and 'charlatte' appear for recipes with chopped pork or veal cooked in sweetened milk of almonds. Special moulds were created in the great eighteenth- and nineteenth-century kitchens for this dish. Traditionally, the bread was fried in clarified butter, but The Pudding Club version uses buttered toast fingers.

 Serves 4-6

2 LB (960G) COOKING APPLES, PEELED, CORED AND SLICED	I TEASPOON MIXED SPICE
2 OZ (60G) BUTTER	AT LEAST 8 THIN SLICES OF BREAD, WITHOUT CRUSTS
6 OZ (180G) SUGAR	4 OZ (120G) BUTTER, MELTED
2 TABLESPOONS LEMON JUICE	I TABLESPOON CASTER SUGAR
I TABLESPOON FINELY GRATED LEMON PEEL	

Preheat the oven to 200°C/400°F/Gas 6.

Simmer the apples gently in a pan until soft with the butter, sugar, lemon juice, lemon peel and mixed spice. Toast the bread then brush with melted butter, and cut into fingers. Line a deep 2 pint (1.1 litre) ovenproof dish completely with the bread fingers, pressing the buttered sides against the dish. Pour in the apple and cover the top with more bread strips. Bake for about 30 minutes, or until the top is crisp and brown. Turn out carefully, and sprinkle with the caster sugar. It looks like a buttery brown loaf full of soft fragrant apples. Serve with cream, custard or golden syrup.

Apple Dappy

This pudding starts as a Swiss roll filled with apples spiced with cinnamon, and is baked in whirligig slices in a syrupy lemon sauce.

 Serves 4-6

8 OZ (240G) SELF-RAISING FLOUR	I LB (480G) COOKING APPLES,
I TEASPOON BAKING POWDER	PEELED, CORED AND CHOPPED
2 OZ (60G) BUTTER OR MARGARINE	I TABLESPOON DEMERARA SUGAR
¼ PINT (150ML) MILK	½ TEASPOON GROUND ALLSPICE
	OR POWDERED CINNAMON

Lemon syrup

I LEMON	4 OZ (120G) SUGAR
I TABLESPOON GOLDEN SYRUP	7 FL OZ (200ML) WATER
½ OZ (15G) BUTTER OR MARGARINE	

Preheat the oven to 190°C/375°F/Gas 5.

Make the lemon syrup first. Peel the lemon as thinly as possible and squeeze the juice out. Put the rind, juice and other ingredients into a pan and heat gently, stirring until the sugar is dissolved. Leave to stand until needed.

Sieve the flour and baking powder into a large mixing bowl and rub in the butter or margarine until the mixture resembles fine crumbs. Mix to a dough with the milk. Roll out on to a floured board to about 8 in (20cm) square and approximately ¼ in (5mm) thick. Spread the chopped apples on the pastry, sprinkle with sugar and spice and roll up the pastry and apple like a Swiss roll. Cut into 1 in (2.5cm) slices and arrange in a greased 2 pint (1.1 litre) ovenproof dish. Remove the rind from the syrup and pour over the slices. Bake for 30 minutes or until it puffs up golden brown. Serve with custard.

Apricot Cap Sponge Pudding

This pudding looks very pretty when turned out, as the apricots give a layered effect like tiles on a roof. It is good cold too, as the apricots jelly slightly. Nowadays most preserved apricots no longer need soaking, but the dried varieties from health-food shops do.

 Serves 4-6

10 OZ (300G) DRIED OR PRESERVED APRICOTS	2 LARGE EGGS, BEATEN
DEMERARA SUGAR	8 OZ (240G) SELF-RAISING FLOUR
6 OZ (180G) BUTTER	FINELY GRATED RIND OF 1 LEMON
6 OZ (180G) CASTER SUGAR	ABOUT 4 TABLESPOONS MILK

Soak 8 oz (240g) of the apricots overnight in cold water (if necessary), reserving the remaining 2 oz (60g). Grease a 2 pint (1.1 litre) pudding basin, and coat with demerara sugar. Drain the apricots and place them flesh side over the sugar to line the basin from the base upwards. Finely shred the remaining 2 oz (60g) apricots with a sharp knife. Cream the butter and sugar together until light and fluffy, then beat in the eggs. Sieve the flour, and fold into the mixture, along with the shredded apricots and lemon rind. Add enough of the milk to give a dropping consistency. Spoon into the basin, taking care not to dislodge the apricots. Cover securely and steam for 1½-2 hours until light and spongy. Turn out and serve with crème fraîche, Greek yoghurt, cream or custard.

Orange and Coconut Pudding

Slices of peeled orange in overlapping rings laid on brown sugar make a juicy and attractive topping.

 Serves 4-6

3 OZ (90G) BUTTER OR MARGARINE	3 OZ (90G) DESICCATED COCONUT
2 EGGS, BEATEN	3 TABLESPOONS FRESH ORANGE
6 OZ (180G) SELF-RAISING FLOUR	JUICE
3 OZ (90G) SUGAR	

Grease a 2 pint (1.1 litre) pudding basin. Beat the butter or margarine to a cream, then add the beaten egg, sieved flour, sugar, coconut and orange juice. Mix well together. Place in the basin, cover securely and steam for 1½ hours. Serve with Orange Sauce, preferably the one with Cointreau (see page 123).

St Clement's Pudding

This orange-flavoured pudding with lemon sauce gets its name from the old nursery rhyme, 'Oranges and lemons, say the bells of St Clement's.'

 Serves 4-6

4 OZ (120G) BUTTER	4 OZ (120G) SELF-RAISING FLOUR
4 OZ (120G) CASTER SUGAR	2 EGGS, BEATEN
JUICE AND FINELY GRATED RIND	2 TABLESPOONS MARMALADE
OF I ORANGE	

Cream the butter and sugar together until light and fluffy. Mix in the orange juice and rind. Beat in the sifted flour and beaten egg a little at a time. Put the marmalade in the bottom of a greased 2 pint (1.1 litre) basin, and pour the mixture on top. Cover securely and steam for 1½–2 hours. Serve with Lemon Sauce (see page 122) or custard.

Apple Surprise

In this recipe the sauce is poured over the pudding mixture; it soaks through and then appears underneath – a nice surprise – when baked in the oven.

 Serves 4-6

4 OZ (120G) PLAIN FLOUR	8 OZ (240G) SOFT BROWN SUGAR
2 TEASPOONS BAKING POWDER	2 OZ (60G) BUTTER
1 TABLESPOON SUGAR	1 TABLESPOON LEMON JUICE
1 COOKING APPLE, PEELED, CORED AND CHOPPED	16 FL OZ (500ML) BOILING WATER
	½ TEASPOON POWDERED CINNAMON
4 FL OZ (125ML) MILK	

Preheat the oven to 180°C/350°F/Gas 4.

Sift together the flour, baking powder and sugar. Add the apple pieces and mix with the milk. Put into a greased 2 pint (1.1 litre) pie dish. Mix together the brown sugar, butter, lemon juice and boiling water and pour over the pudding. Finally sprinkle with cinnamon and bake for 25 minutes. Serve with custard or cream.

Sticky Pear Pudding

This pudding is an upside-down one, made with either fresh or tinned pears. It is important to use a pudding basin of china or glass, not plastic, because it is baked in the oven, not steamed.

 Serves 4-6

2 LARGE PEARS, OR A 220G TIN OF HALVED PEARS	4 OZ (120G) SUGAR
	2 EGGS, BEATEN
5 OZ (150G) BUTTER	5 OZ (150G) SELF-RAISING FLOUR
3 OZ (90G) DEMERARA SUGAR	2 TABLESPOONS MILK
2 TABLESPOONS GOLDEN SYRUP	

Preheat the oven to 190°C/375°F/Gas 5.

Peel the fresh pears, remove the cores and cut into 1/3in (1cm) thick slices lengthways. Cut the tinned pears similarly. Poach the fresh pears gently in a little boiling water for 3 minutes (add the juice of a lemon for extra flavour). Melt 1 oz (30g) of the butter, the demerara sugar and the syrup in a pan and cook gently until the sugar dissolves. Pour the caramel mixture over the bottom and sides of a greased 2 pint (1.1 litre) pudding basin or mould. Arrange the pear slices over the sides and base, pressing them firmly into the caramel. Beat the remaining butter and the sugar together until light and fluffy. Beat in the eggs gradually, then stir in the flour and milk. Spoon the sponge mixture into the basin and level the surface. Bake for about 1 hour or until firm to the touch and golden brown. Turn out carefully and serve with custard.

Cinnamon and Banana Sponge Pudding

Bananas give a good texture and flavour to a spiced sponge mixture.

 Serves 4

4 OZ (120G) MARGARINE	1½ LEVEL TEASPOONS POWDERED
4 OZ (120G) SUGAR	CINNAMON
1 LARGE EGG, BEATEN	2 BANANAS, PEELED
1 TABLESPOON MILK	2 TEASPOONS LEMON JUICE
4 OZ (120G) SELF-RAISING FLOUR	
½ LEVEL TEASPOON BAKING POWDER	

Cream the margarine and sugar together, then beat in the egg and milk. Sift the flour, baking powder and cinnamon together. Mash the bananas with the lemon juice, then stir into the creamed mixture and fold in the flour. Spoon into a greased 1½ pint (900 ml) pudding basin, cover securely, and steam for 1 hour. Turn out and serve with custard.

Summer Pudding

The excuse for including this one cold dessert is that it is so delicious, so famous and so British.

Traditionally the filling was raspberries and redcurrants, but any mixture of soft fruits can be used as they are available. However, a mixture of strawberries, raspberries, gooseberries, red- and blackcurrants and finely chopped rhubarb is especially good. As the seasons for all these fruits overlap for only a few weeks, this becomes a special pudding not to be missed. The fruit mixture can be frozen or bottled, but it is not as sparklingly flavoursome as fresh.

Serves 4-6

1½ LB (720G) MIXED FRUIT	6-8 LARGE SLICES WHITE BREAD,
(SEE ABOVE)	½ IN (1.25CM) THICK, CRUSTS
SUGAR TO TASTE	REMOVED

Make the filling first. Cook the mixed fruits in a pan in a very little water until soft, then add sugar to taste. Completely line a greased 2 pint (1.1 litre) basin with most of the bread. (Tailor the bread as necessary.) Pour in the boiling fruit and cover with the remaining bread, cut to fit. Place a small plate on top of the bread, and stand a heavy weight on it so that the juice is absorbed by the bread, turning it a wonderful rich colour. Leave in a cold place until needed. Turn out very carefully, and serve with cream.

CHAPTER THREE

Regional Round-up

Puddings are traditional and appreciated through the whole of Britain, and there is a wealth of regional diversity. Sometimes, though, it would appear that language does not 'travel' quite so well.

We were somewhat taken aback a few years ago when a disc-jockey from Radio Glasgow, in the middle of a live transmission, rang to tell us that it was time for us, as founders of The Pudding Club, and for all Sassenachs, to be made aware that in Scotland the phrase 'in The Pudding Club' meant a lot more than it did in England. 'It means – chuckle, chuckle – get this – chuckle, chuckle – that you're pregnant! You didna know that, did you?' he demanded. 'Crumbs!' was all we could muster by way of response, although we did remember to thank him for the information and admit that we were uncertain whether or not we dared drop this bombshell on our English membership. . .

Sussex Pond Pudding

Some brisk correspondence exists in the archives over this pudding. Purists declare the addition of a lemon to be the 'twentieth-century whim of a seriously misguided cook', and furthermore 'the pudding dating from the seventeenth century is served with roast Southdown lamb, the pudding crust dotted with currants, the centre oozing with butter and sugar.'

 ## Serves 8

8 OZ (240G) SELF-RAISING FLOUR	4 OZ (120G) BUTTER
A PINCH OF SALT	4 OZ (120G) DEMERARA SUGAR
4 OZ (120G) SHREDDED SUET	I LARGE LEMON
ABOUT ¼ PINT (150ML) MILK AND	
WATER MIXED	

Sieve the flour and salt into a mixing bowl, then add the suet and mix well. Add the liquid to make a soft dough which can be rolled out. It is very important that the dough is not too wet or thin. Grease a 2½-3 pint (1.4-1.7 litre) pudding basin. Roll the dough into a large circle and cut out a quarter to use later for making a lid. Place the remaining dough in the basin and join up the two cuts, wetting the edges, so that the basin is completely lined.

Cut the butter into small pieces and put half in the basin with half the sugar. Prick the whole lemon (preferably one with a thin skin) all over, using a thick skewer. Place on top of the butter and sugar in the basin. Cover with the rest of the butter and sugar.

Roll out the remaining pastry to make a lid. Fit over the filling, and press the edges together with water to seal them firmly. Cover securely and steam for 3½ hours, or longer (for a really tender lemon), adding more water if needed.

To serve, turn the pudding into a dish with a deep rim. (It may not hold to shape as well as other puddings.) When you slice into it, the rich lemon-flavoured sauce will gush out. The lemon is the frog in the pond. Make sure each person is served some of the suet crust, lemon and tangy luscious sauce.

Kentish Well Pudding

Make the suet crust as for Sussex Pond Pudding, but use this filling.

I TABLESPOON GOLDEN SYRUP	4 OZ (120G) BUTTER
JUICE AND FINELY GRATED RIND	4 OZ (120G) SOFT BROWN SUGAR
OF I LEMON	5 OZ (120G) CURRANTS

 Place the golden syrup in the bottom of the greased basin with some shreds of lemon rind before lining with suet pastry. Mix together the ingredients for the filling, and place in the lined basin. Cover with the pastry top, press together, then cover securely and steam as before. Turn out and serve with custard.

Hampshire Six-Cup Pudding

The joy of this famous regional pudding is that a cup is used to measure the ingredients – the size does not matter, just so long as the same size cup is used throughout. As we've said before, the larger the cup, the bigger the pudding!

 Serves 4-6

I CUP PLAIN FLOUR	I CUP SOFT BROWN SUGAR
A PINCH OF SALT	I CUP MIXED DRIED FRUIT
I CUP BREADCRUMBS	I TEASPOON BICARBONATE OF SODA
I CUP SHREDDED SUET	I CUP MILK, WARMED

Sift the flour, then mix together with all the dry ingredients down to the fruit. Stir the bicarbonate of soda into the warm milk, then add to the dry ingredients. Put into a greased 2 pint (1.1 litre) pudding basin, cover securely, and steam for 4 hours. Turn out and serve with custard.

Helston Pudding

A delicious light-textured fruit pudding originating from Helston in Cornwall. It can be made in advance, freezes well and can be used as a light alternative to Christmas pudding.

 Serves 4-6

2 OZ (60G) SELF-RAISING FLOUR	2 OZ (60G) SOFT BROWN SUGAR
A PINCH OF SALT	3 OZ (90G) SHREDDED SUET
2 OZ (60G) GROUND RICE	1 TEASPOON GROUND NUTMEG
2 OZ (60G) BROWN BREADCRUMBS	¼ TEASPOON BICARBONATE OF
2 OZ (60G) RAISINS OR SULTANAS	SODA
2 OZ (60G) CURRANTS	MILK TO MIX
2 OZ (60G) DRIED APRICOTS,	
CHOPPED	

Sieve the flour and salt together, then mix all the dry ingredients in a large bowl. Add enough milk to form a soft dropping consistency, then put into a well-greased 2 pint (1.1 litre) pudding basin. Cover securely and steam for 2 hours. Serve with clotted cream, or a Rich White Sauce (see page 126) flavoured with a little brandy.

Cumberland Rum Pudding

Cinnamon, cocoa and rum are the three simple ingredients that make this steamed sponge pudding so delectable and luxurious.

 Serves 8

12 OZ (360G) SELF-RAISING FLOUR	2 TABLESPOONS HOT WATER
5 OZ (150G) BUTTER OR MARGARINE	5 OZ (150G) CASTER SUGAR
1 ROUNDED TABLESPOON COCOA	1 EGG, BEATEN
POWDER	2 TABLESPOONS MILK

Filling

2 OZ (60G) BUTTER, SOFTENED	1 OZ (30G) RAISINS
4 OZ (120G) SOFT BROWN SUGAR	½ LEVEL TEASPOON POWDERED
1 TABLESPOON RUM, OR FINELY	CINNAMON
GRATED RIND AND JUICE OF	
½ ORANGE	

Sieve the flour into a large mixing bowl. Rub the butter or margarine into the flour to form fine crumbs. Blend the cocoa with the hot water and add to the flour mixture with the sugar, beaten egg and milk. Beat until smooth. Place two-thirds of the mixture into a greased 2 pint (1.1 litre) pudding basin. With the back of a spoon, spread it evenly over the base and sides to within 1 in (2.5cm) of the top of the basin, leaving a hollow in the middle.

Place all the filling ingredients into a bowl and beat until smooth and well mixed. Place the filling in the hollow, and smooth over. Spread the remaining sponge mixture over the filling. Cover securely and steam for 1½ hours. Turn out and serve with lashings of custard.

For Apple Dappy, a pastry dough encases the fruit filling like a Swiss roll, then is cut into slices before baking. See page 52.

 The only pudding in the book which is not steamed or baked, Summer Pudding is such a British classic, it could not be omitted. See page 58.

The mixture for the very traditional College Pudding
can also be deep-fried as dumplings.
See page 67.

St Nicholas Pudding is made with plums and
served with its own special plum sauce.
See page 80.

Serve Pineapple and Coconut Pudding hot with
custard or cold with cream.
See page 86.

Chocolate Pudding with Fudgenut Chocolate Topping
is sheer indulgence for chocolate lovers.
See page 90.

Upside-down Winter Fruit Pudding is a steamed
sponge decorated lavishly with dried fruit.
See page 91.

 Made with marmalade and apricots, Lord Randall's Pudding
is one of the most consistent winners at PC evenings.
See page 94.

Ascot Pudding

The recipe from The Pudding Club archive does not identify whether this pudding is connected with the town of Ascot, or with its racecourse; nevertheless it is a very fine pudding served with its own sauce, or custard.

 ## Serves 4-6

3 OZ (90G) PUDDING RICE	1 OZ (30G) MIXED PEEL
1¼ PINTS (700ML) MILK	6 OZ (180G) SULTANAS
3 OZ (90G) SHREDDED SUET	3 EGGS, BEATEN AND STRAINED
3 OZ (90G) SUGAR	

Sauce

8 FL OZ (250ML) SHERRY OR WHITE WINE	3 EGG YOLKS
	1 TEASPOON LEMON JUICE
1½ OZ (45G) SUGAR	

Cook the rice gently in the milk until it is tender and all the milk has been absorbed. Let it cool then mix with the suet, sugar, mixed peel, sultanas and the beaten strained eggs. Put the mixture into a well greased 2 pint (1.1 litre) pudding basin and cover securely. Steam for 3 hours, and turn out.

To make the sauce, heat the wine and dissolve the sugar in it. While still hot, stir in the beaten egg yolks. Put this sauce in a double saucepan, and stir until it thickens like custard. Do not let it boil, lest it curdle. Add the lemon juice. Pour the sauce over the pudding, or serve separately in a sauce boat.

Oxford Pudding

This pudding's connection with Oxford probably derives from the famous brand of marmalade made there.

 Serves 4-6

2 OZ (60G) SOFT BROWN SUGAR	4 OZ (120G) GOLDEN SYRUP
6 OZ (180G) SELF-RAISING FLOUR	4 OZ (120G) THICK MARMALADE
A PINCH OF SALT	I EGG, BEATEN
2 OZ (60G) GROUND RICE	2 TABLESPOONS MILK
4 OZ (120G) SHREDDED SUET	

Grease a 2 pint (1.1 litre) pudding basin, and press the sugar round the sides and the base. Sift the flour and salt together and then add the rice. Stir in the shredded suet, golden syrup and marmalade, and then add the beaten egg and milk mixed together. Turn into the basin, cover securely and steam for 3 hours. Turn out and serve with warmed syrup and custard.

College Pudding

Traditionally this pudding was served to students in the college halls of Oxford and Cambridge. There is a variation from New College Oxford, which consists of this mixture being dropped into hot oil, fried for 3 minutes, then dusted with caster sugar. (Incidentally, this is a useful way to cook almost any pudding when time is short.)

 Serves 4-6

3 OZ (90G) SELF-RAISING FLOUR	1 OZ (30G) CANDIED PEEL,
A PINCH OF SALT	CHOPPED
3 OZ (90G) BREADCRUMBS	2 OZ (60G) SOFT BROWN SUGAR
3 OZ (90G) SHREDDED SUET	1 EGG, BEATEN
3 OZ (90G) RAISINS	6 TABLESPOONS MILK
2 OZ (60G) CURRANTS	

Sift the flour and salt together, then mix with all the remaining dry ingredients. Beat the egg and add to the dry ingredients with enough of the milk to produce a soft dropping consistency. Spoon into a greased 2 pint (1.1 litre) pudding basin, cover securely and steam for 2½ hours. This pudding turns out easily if left for a few minutes after taking it out of the steamer. Turn out and serve with custard.

Cloutie Dumpling

Credited with giving Scotsman the stamina to get through Hogmanay, this is a very substantial pudding. The word 'cloutie' means cloth, in which the 'dumpling' was boiled. Another name is 'bag pudding'.

 Serves 8

12 OZ (360G) SELF-RAISING FLOUR	I SMALL COOKING APPLE, PEELED, CORED AND GRATED
½ TEASPOON SALT	
3 OZ (90G) CASTER SUGAR	I MEDIUM CARROT, GRATED
3 OZ (90G) SHREDDED SUET	¾ TABLESPOON BLACK TREACLE
3 OZ (90G) BREADCRUMBS	2 TABLESPOONS DARK RUM
6 OZ (180G) CURRANTS	(OPTIONAL)
8 OZ (240G) RAISINS	ABOUT 7 FL OZ (200ML) MILK
I TEASPOON MIXED SPICE	

Mix the dry ingredients in a large bowl. Add the grated apple and carrot. Dissolve the treacle in 1 tablespoon of hot water and add to the mixture, with the rum if using. Add enough milk to bind the mixture to a soft consistency (but be careful, not too soft). This should be boiled in a pudding cloth (see page 18), but can also be steamed in a greased 3 pint (1.7 litre) pudding basin, covered securely, for 3 hours. Turn out and serve with custard.

A Lighter Cloutie Dumpling

This cloutie dumpling recipe is easier to make and lighter on the digestion.

 Serves 8

12 OZ (360G) SELF-RAISING FLOUR	1 LB (480G) SULTANAS
½ TEASPOON SALT	8 OZ (240G) CURRANTS
6 OZ (180G) BUTTER	1 TABLESPOON GOLDEN SYRUP
4 OZ (120G) SOFT BROWN SUGAR	1 TABLESPOON BLACK TREACLE
1 TEASPOON POWDERED CINNAMON	2 EGGS, BEATEN
1 TEASPOON GROUND GINGER	MILK TO MIX
FINELY GRATED RIND OF 1 ORANGE	

Sieve the flour and salt together into a large bowl, then rub the butter in until the mixture resembles crumbs. Mix with all the remaining dry ingredients. Make a well in the mixture and add the syrup, treacle, eggs and enough milk to make a stiff but moist mixture. Spoon into a greased 3 pint (1.7 litre) pudding basin, cover securely and steam for 3 hours. Turn out and serve with custard or a Rich White Sauce (see page 126).

Bakewell Pudding

A famous pudding that has stood the test of time and is still made by bakeries. Like many successful recipes, it appears to be the result of a happy accident. The cook at the Rutland Arms at Bakewell in Derbyshire, so the story goes, made a mistake with the recipe, and ended up with a cross between a pudding and a cake. A similar pudding in the southern counties is known as Alderman's Pudding.

 Serves 4-6

Pastry

6 OZ (180G) SELF-RAISING FLOUR	1½ OZ (45G) LARD
1½ OZ (45G) MARGARINE	COLD WATER TO MIX

Filling

2 HEAPED TABLESPOONS APRICOT JAM	3 OZ (90G) CASTER SUGAR
	4 OZ (120G) BUTTER, MELTED
3 EGGS, BEATEN	3 OZ (90G) GROUND ALMONDS

Preheat the oven to 200°C/400°F/Gas 6.

Make the pastry by rubbing the flour and fats together to fine crumbs. Add enough water to make a rolling dough. Wrap and chill for half an hour, then roll out to ¼ in (5mm) thick.

Line a deep 8 in (20cm) pie dish with the pastry. Warm the jam and spread it evenly over the pastry base. Beat the eggs and sugar together until light and creamy, then stir in the melted butter and ground almonds and pour over the jam. Bake for 25-30 minutes or until the filling is set. Serve with custard.

Snowdon Pudding

A marmalade-flavoured pudding served as a traditional treat to climbers of this famous Welsh mountain. A few halves of glacé cherries and raisins scattered in the bottom of the basin give a dash of colour when turned out. Line the basin with a round of greaseproof paper first.

Serves 4-6

8 OZ (240G) BREADCRUMBS	FINELY GRATED RIND OF 2 LEMONS
2 OZ (60G) GROUND RICE	AND A LITTLE LEMON JUICE
4 OZ (120G) SHREDDED SUET	2 EGGS, BEATEN
4 OZ (120G) RAISINS OR SULTANAS	¼ PINT (150ML) MILK
4 OZ (120G) SUGAR	3 TABLESPOONS MARMALADE
A PINCH OF SALT	

Mix the dry ingredients and lemon rind together in a large bowl. Beat the eggs with the milk and add to the bowl with a little lemon juice. Mix well, then add the marmalade and turn into a greased 2 pint (1.1 litre) pudding basin. Cover securely and steam for 3 hours. Serve with a Rich White Sauce (see page 126) which, when poured over the pudding, resembles snow on a mountain.

Battersea Pudding

A delicious pudding, with the apples rising to the surface through billowing golden batter.

 Serves 4-6

3 COOKING APPLES, PEELED, CORED AND SLICED	A PINCH OF SALT
SUGAR TO TASTE	2 EGGS, BEATEN
4 OZ (120G) PLAIN FLOUR	6 OZ (175ML) MILK
	2 OZ (60G) SHREDDED SUET

Preheat the oven to 180°C/350°F/Gas 4.

Grease an 8 in (20cm) ovenproof dish, line with the sliced apples, and sprinkle with sugar to taste. Sift the flour and salt together in a bowl, and make a well in the middle. Gradually beat in the beaten eggs and the milk until the consistency of a Yorkshire pudding batter. (This benefits from standing for about 20 minutes.) Pour the batter over the apples. Scatter the suet over the top of the pudding and bake in the oven for 30-45 minutes, making sure that it is well browned. The apples will have risen to the surface. Serve with cream or custard.

The pudding can be reheated successfully, and is good for using up extra Yorkshire pudding batter.

Irish Black Pudding

Not a traditional savoury black pudding, but a sweet one, combining candied peel, cream and Irish whiskey with breadcrumbs, suet, and other flavourings. It is not very black, but a sprinkling of currants in the bottom of the basin makes a nice dark topping.

 Serves 6-8

8 OZ (240G) BREADCRUMBS	4 OZ (120G) SUGAR
4 OZ (120G) SHREDDED SUET	½ TEASPOON MIXED SPICE
4 OZ (120G) CURRANTS	2 EGGS, SEPARATED
2 OZ (60G) GROUND ALMONDS	I TABLESPOON IRISH WHISKEY
2 OZ (60G) CANDIED PEEL, CHOPPED	½ PINT (300ML) SINGLE CREAM

Mix all the dry ingredients together. Beat the egg whites until stiff. Beat the egg yolks and mix with the whiskey and the cream. Add this to the dry ingredients and then gently fold in the whipped egg whites. Turn into a well-greased 2 pint (1.1 litre) pudding basin, cover securely and steam for 3 hours. Turn out and serve with custard.

Sir Watkin Williams Wynne's Pudding

The origins of this pudding stem from a Welsh Border family who ran a pack of foxhounds. The original recipe contained beef marrow instead of suet.

 Serves 4-6

2 OZ (60G) SELF-RAISING FLOUR	3 TABLESPOONS ORANGE OR
A PINCH OF SALT	LEMON MARMALADE
6 OZ (180G) BREADCRUMBS	3 EGGS, BEATEN
4 OZ (120G) SHREDDED SUET	I TABLESPOON RUM OR BRANDY
3 OZ (90G) SUGAR	JUICE OF ½ LARGE LEMON

Sift the flour and salt together, then add the remaining ingredients, and mix thoroughly. Turn into a greased 2 pint (1.1 litre) pudding basin, covering securely and steam for 3 hours. Turn out and serve with custard or Brandy Butter (see page 121).

CHAPTER FOUR

Festive Occasions

THE WONDERFUL puddings here have something more elaborate in their ingredients or preparation – enough to make them suitable for a special occasion and provide ample justification for the extra cost or extra work. Included here is the steamed pudding with which everyone in Britain is familiar – the Christmas pudding. Although its origins are very traditionally British, it only became a national institution during Victorian times.

Often meetings of The Pudding Club themselves become occasions to make a celebration, whether it be Uncle George's seventieth birthday ('Uncle George loves his puddings, you know') or John and Susan announcing to their friends that they are happily expectant. On one particularly memorable occasion Keith welcomed a coachload of ladies to a meeting of The Pudding Club and enquired, jokingly, if this was a meeting of Weight Watchers. 'That's right,' they said, 'it's an end-of-term celebration!'

The Pudding Club's Christmas Pudding

This is the Christmas pudding most popular with Pudding Club members. The recipe makes two puddings. Try and make them a few weeks ahead of the big day, as they improve with keeping. The Sunday before Advent, Stir-up Sunday, is the traditional pudding mixing day.

 Serves 4-6

2½ LB (1.2KG) MIXED DRIED FRUIT	4 OZ (120G) GLACÉ CHERRIES
8 OZ (240G) READY-SOAKED PRUNES, CHOPPED	1 LARGE CARROT, PEELED AND GRATED
8 OZ (240G) BREADCRUMBS	4 OZ (120G) GROUND ALMONDS
2 LARGE COOKING APPLES, PEELED, CHOPPED AND GRATED	4 OZ (120G) PLAIN FLOUR
2 OZ (60G) BLANCHED ALMONDS, CHOPPED	½ TEASPOON POWDERED CINNAMON
	½ TEASPOON GROUND NUTMEG
1 TEASPOON MIXED SPICE	8 OZ (240G) SHREDDED SUET
FINELY GRATED RIND AND JUICE OF 1 LEMON AND 1 ORANGE	1 TEASPOON SALT
	½ CAN STOUT
	1 SHERRY GLASS BRANDY
8 OZ (240G) SOFT BROWN SUGAR	3 EGGS, BEATEN

Mix all the ingredients together, give a good stir – make sure the family wish during the stirring – and leave to stand overnight. Turn into two 2 pint (1.1 litre) pudding basins, filling right to the top, or one 4 pint (2.3 litre) basin. Cover securely and steam the small ones for 6 hours and a large one for 10 hours. To reheat, steam the small ones for about 1 hour, the larger for 2 hours. Serve with Brandy Butter (see page 121).

A Christmas Pudding Without Fat

A tasty and light alternative Christmas pudding.

 Serves 4-6

12 OZ (360G) BROWN BREADCRUMBS	8 OZ (240G) SOFT BROWN SUGAR
I LARGE COOKING APPLE, PEELED,	3 TEASPOONS MIXED SPICE
CORED AND SLICED	I TEASPOON SALT
I BANANA, PEELED AND SLICED	JUICE AND FINELY GRATED RIND
4 OZ (120G) SHELLED BRAZIL NUTS	OF I LEMON
I OZ (30G) BLANCHED ALMONDS	½ PINT (300ML) MILK
8 OZ (240G) CURRANTS	3 EGGS, BEATEN
8 OZ (240G) SULTANAS	

Liquidise the first five ingredients, or chop finely in a food processor. Put in a bowl with the rest of the ingredients. Mix together thoroughly, then put in a greased 3 pint (1.7 litre) pudding basin. Cover securely and steam for 6 hours. Turn out and serve with Rich White Sauce or Brandy Butter (see pages 126 and 121).

A Modern Christmas Pudding

This pudding is included because it can be cooked in that remarkable piece of technology, the microwave oven. The timings given below are for an 800w microwave oven.

Serves 10

3 OZ (90G) PLAIN FLOUR	3 OZ (90G) RAISINS
¼ TEASPOON SALT	4 OZ (120G) SULTANAS
3 OZ (90G) SHREDDED SUET	1½ OZ (45G) BLANCHED ALMONDS,
½ TEASPOON MIXED SPICE	CHOPPED
¼ TEASPOON POWDERED CINNAMON	2 OZ (30G) APPLE, PEELED, CORED
1½ OZ (45G) BREADCRUMBS	AND CHOPPED
2 OZ (60G) CASTER SUGAR	JUICE AND FINELY GRATED RIND
2 OZ (60G) CANDIED PEEL,	OF ½ LEMON
CHOPPED	2 TEASPOONS GOLDEN SYRUP
2 OZ (60G) DARK SOFT BROWN	2 TEASPOONS GRAVY BROWNING
SUGAR	4 TABLESPOONS BRANDY
2 OZ (60G) GLACÉ CHERRIES,	2 EGGS, BEATEN
CHOPPED	2 FL OZ (60ML) MILK
3 OZ (90G) CURRANTS	

Sift the flour and salt together, and then mix all the dry ingredients down to and including the apple and lemon rind together. Stir in all the remaining ingredients, and place the pudding mixture in a greased 3 pint (1.7 litre) pudding basin. Cover securely with a lid and cook in the microwave for 5 minutes. Leave for 5 minutes. Cook for a further 5 minutes. Stand for another 5 minutes. Keep in the refrigerator until needed.

To reheat, remove the pudding from the basin and sprinkle

with 1½ teaspoons water. Cover with cling film and cook in the microwave for 4 minutes. Leave for 4 minutes and then cook for another 3 minutes. Serve with Brandy Butter or a Rich White Sauce (see pages 121 and 126).

Figgy Pudding

Traditionally this pudding is served either on Mothering Sunday, over Easter or at Christmas. Because there is a recipe for a fig pudding to be found in the works of Herodotus, the 'father of history', it is sometimes called after him. The use of figs make this a very solid pudding, and therefore popular with those who like their puddings substantial.

 Serves 4-6

4 OZ (120G) PLAIN FLOUR	8 OZ (240G) DRIED FIGS, CHOPPED
A PINCH OF SALT	FINELY GRATED RIND AND JUICE
4 OZ (120G) BREADCRUMBS	OF 1 LEMON
4 OZ (120G) SHREDDED SUET	2 TABLESPOONS MILK
1 TEASPOON MIXED SPICE	2 EGGS, BEATEN
1 TEASPOON BAKING POWDER	
3 OZ (90G) DARK SOFT BROWN SUGAR	

Sift the flour and salt together, then mix with all the remaining dry ingredients. Add the figs, lemon rind and juice, milk and beaten eggs, then beat well. The mixture should be a soft dropping consistency. Put into a greased 2 pint (1.1 litre) pudding basin, cover securely, and steam for 3 hours. Serve with heated golden syrup and custard.

St Nicholas Pudding

This lovely light fruity plum pudding uses fresh plums, often available from greengrocers and supermarkets even during the winter, but tinned plums may be substituted.

Serves 4-6

4 OZ (120G) BUTTER	6 OZ (180G) PLUMS, STONED
4 OZ (120G) CASTER SUGAR	2 OZ (60G) PRUNES, STONED AND
FINELY GRATED RIND AND JUICE	CHOPPED
OF I ORANGE	I TEASPOON POWDERED CINNAMON
2 EGGS, LIGHTLY BEATEN	2 TABLESPOONS GOLDEN SYRUP
3 OZ (90G) SELF-RAISING FLOUR	6 PLUMS OR PRUNES, HALVED AND
2 OZ (60G) BREADCRUMBS	STONED TO DECORATE

Plum sauce

1½ LB (720G) PLUMS	WATER
8 OZ (240G) SUGAR	

Cream the butter and sugar together until light and fluffy, then add the grated orange rind. Add the eggs gradually to the butter mixture. Sift the flour, mix with the breadcrumbs and fold into the mixture. Stir in the fruit, orange juice and cinnamon. Coat the bottom of a greased 2 pint (1.1 litre) pudding basin with the syrup, and arrange the halves of plums or prunes on top in a circle. Carefully spoon the mixture into the basin. Cover securely and steam for 1¾-2 hours.

Meanwhile, for the sauce, cover the bottom of a saucepan with a little water, and slice the plums into it. Cook at a gentle simmer to prevent sticking. Remove stones, then purée the cooked plums in a blender before sieving. In a separate pan, dissolve the sugar slowly with 4-5 tablespoons water. When the sugar is dissolved, stop stirring and turn the heat up to full. Boil until golden brown and then remove from the heat. Stir in 6 tablespoons water, but carefully, because the mixture spits. Put back on a low heat until the lumps have dissolved. Add the plum purée, and cool a little. (Add a small amount of port or Kirsch if you like.) Turn the pudding out and serve with its special plum sauce poured over.

Duchess's Pudding

This delicate light fruit and nut pudding would tempt even the most diet-conscious Duchess.

 Serves 4-6

4 OZ (120G) BUTTER	1 OZ (30G) SHELLED WALNUTS,
4 OZ (120G) CASTER SUGAR	CHOPPED
2 EGGS, BEATEN	3-4 DROPS ALMOND ESSENCE
5 OZ (150G) SELF-RAISING FLOUR	MILK TO MIX
2 OZ (60G) MIXED DRIED FRUIT	
1 OZ (30G) GLACÉ CHERRIES,	
CHOPPED	

Cream the butter and sugar together until light and fluffy. Gradually add the eggs to the creamed mixture, beating them in well. Sift the flour into the mixture, then add the fruit, nuts, almond essence and enough milk to give it a soft dropping consistency. Put into a greased 2 pint (1.1 litre) pudding basin and steam for 1½-2 hours. Serve with custard or Lemon Sauce (see page 122).

Marlborough Pudding

The Elizabethans perfected the pudding pie, of which this seems to be an example, with a custard filling contained in a rim of puff pastry. This version has sponge cakes in the bottom. It needs to be eaten straight from the oven.

6 OZ (180G) PUFF PASTRY	6 OZ (180G) BUTTER
3 SMALL TRIFLE SPONGES	3 OZ (90G) SUGAR
2 TABLESPOONS MARMALADE	4 EGG YOLKS
FINELY GRATED RIND AND JUICE	2 EGG WHITES
OF 1 LEMON	

Preheat the oven to 150°C/300°F/Gas 2.

Roll the pastry to ¼ in (5mm) thick, and cut into strips that will fit the sides of a 10 in (25cm) square dish. Grease the dish, then line the sides with these strips. Crumble the sponge cakes into the dish. Warm the marmalade with the lemon juice, and pour over the sponge cakes. Cream the butter and sugar with the grated lemon rind, beating until white and fluffy. Stir in the egg yolks, and fold in the stiffly whipped egg whites. Pour this mixture over the sponge cakes and bake for approximately 45 minutes or until golden brown. Serve with custard.

Prince Albert Pudding

A pudding surrounded by dark succulent prunes, named after Queen Victoria's consort, Prince Albert. The lighter mixture of ground rice and no suet probably suited his preference for plain food, and the beneficial effects of prunes were well appreciated in Victorian times. . .

 ## Serves 4-6

9 OZ (270G) READY-SOAKED PRUNES	1½ OZ (45G) GROUND RICE
2 OZ (60G) BUTTER, MELTED	4 OZ (120G) BROWN BREADCRUMBS
4 OZ (120G) MARGARINE	FINELY GRATED RIND OF 1 LEMON
4 OZ (120G) CASTER SUGAR	MILK TO MIX
3 EGGS, SEPARATED	

Line the base of a 2½ pint (1.4 litre) pudding basin with a round of greaseproof paper. Slice the prunes in half, removing stones if necessary. Dip the prunes in melted butter and use to completely line the basin, placing the fleshy side to the basin. Cream the margarine and sugar together until light and fluffy. Beat the egg yolks into the margarine mixture, then fold in the ground rice, breadcrumbs and lemon rind. Add enough milk to make a soft dropping consistency. Beat the egg whites to a stiff froth, fold into the mixture, and put it carefully into the prune-lined basin. Cover securely and steam for 2½ hours. Turn out and serve with cream or custard.

Tip
This pudding is also good served cold with whipped cream and perhaps some fresh cherries.

Tipsy Pudding

No-one is going to get tipsy, but the brandy sauce soaks through the pudding, giving it a delicious whiff of alcohol.

 Serves 4-6

I TEASPOON BICARBONATE OF SODA	I EGG, BEATEN
8 OZ (240G) STONED DATES, CHOPPED	6 OZ (180G) PLAIN FLOUR
	A PINCH OF SALT
8 FL OZ (250ML) BOILING WATER	¼ TEASPOON BAKING POWDER
2 OZ (60G) BUTTER	4 OZ (120G) SHELLED WALNUTS,
6 OZ (180G) SUGAR	CHOPPED

Sauce

6 OZ (180G) SUGAR	I TEASPOON VANILLA ESSENCE
8 FL OZ (250ML) COLD WATER	I OZ (30G) BUTTER
4 TABLESPOONS BRANDY	

Preheat the oven to 180°C/350°F/Gas 4.

Sprinkle the bicarbonate of soda over the dates, add the boiling water and leave to stand. Cream the butter and sugar together, then add the egg and beat together. Sift the flour, salt and baking powder into the egg mixture and beat well. Add the date mixture with the chopped walnuts. Spread ½-¾ in (1-2cm) thick in a flat greased ovenproof dish, with 2 in (5cm) sides, about 10 in (25cm) square. It is very important that the mixture is not spread too thick. Bake for 30-35 minutes, then cut into squares while still hot.

Meanwhile place the sauce ingredients in a saucepan, bring to the boil and gently boil without a lid for 5 minutes. Pour over the hot pudding and serve.

Aphrodite's Pudding

Quinces are reputed aphrodisiacs, thus their association with the Greek goddess of love. Quinces are generally available during the autumn, and a bowl of them can scent a room. A slice can cheer up an apple pie, while they make a marvellous, albeit labour-intensive marmalade or jelly.

 Serves 4-6

4 OZ (120G) BUTTER	8 OZ (240G) QUINCES, PEELED AND
4 OZ (120G) LIGHT MUSCOVADO	GRATED
SUGAR	1 OZ (30G) FLAKED ALMONDS
½ TEASPOON POWDERED CINNAMON	½ TEASPOON BICARBONATE OF
A PINCH OF GROUND ALLSPICE	SODA DISSOLVED IN 1 TEASPOON
FINELY GRATED ZEST OF 1 ORANGE	WARM WATER
4 OZ (120G) BREADCRUMBS	1 TABLESPOON HONEY OR QUINCE
2 EGGS, BEATEN	JELLY

Cream the butter and sugar together. Mix the spices, zest and breadcrumbs, and add to the butter mixture, alternating with the beaten egg. Mix the quinces with the almonds and add to the mixture. Stir the soda and water into the pudding mixture. Put the honey or quince jelly in the base of a greased 2 pint (1.1 litre) pudding basin and top with the pudding mixture. Cover securely and steam for 1½ hours. Turn out and serve with cream.

Pineapple and Coconut Pudding

This pudding is good hot or cold, and can be reheated in a moderate oven. Serve hot with custard or cold with cream.

 Serves 4-6

Base

4 OZ (120G) PLAIN FLOUR	3 OZ (90G) BUTTER
2 OZ (60G) SOFT BROWN SUGAR	

Mixture

2 EGGS	4 OZ (120G) TINNED OR FRESH
4 OZ (120G) CASTER SUGAR	PINEAPPLE CHUNKS
1 OZ (30G) PLAIN FLOUR	2 OZ (60G) DESICCATED COCONUT
¼ TEASPOON BAKING POWDER	1 OZ (30G) MIXED NUTS, CHOPPED
¼ TEASPOON POWDERED	A FEW DROPS OF VANILLA ESSENCE
CINNAMON	2 OZ (60G) GLACÉ CHERRIES

Preheat the oven to 180°C/350°F/Gas 4.

To make the base, mix the flour and sugar together, then rub in the butter to make fine crumbs. Press into the base of a greased 2 pint (1.1 litre) pie dish. Bake in the oven for 20 minutes.

For the filling, whisk the eggs well, then beat in the sugar until thick. Lightly fold in the flour, baking powder and cinnamon. Drain the pineapple and stir into the mixture with the coconut, nuts and vanilla. Lay the cherries on top of the base, then spread the mixture over them. Bake in the oven (as above) for 50-60 minutes.

Millennium Pudding

A new pudding which was created by Jon George, then chef at Mickleton's Three Ways House Hotel, for the visit of the BBC's Food and Drink Programme in 1997.

 Serves 4-6

8 OZ (240G) SELF-RAISING FLOUR	1 LB (480G) FRESH PEACHES,
A PINCH OF SALT	STONED AND CHOPPED
4 OZ (120G) SHREDDED SUET	1 TABLESPOON BROWN SUGAR
WATER TO MIX	

Syrup

1 LEMON	4 OZ (120G) SOFT BROWN SUGAR
1 TABLESPOON GOLDEN SYRUP	7 FL OZ (200ML) WATER
½ OZ (15G) BUTTER	

Preheat the oven to 190°C/375°F/Gas 5.

Make the syrup first. Peel the lemon as thinly as possible using a swivel peeler, and squeeze out the juice. Put the rind, juice and other ingredients into a pan and heat gently until the sugar is dissolved. Leave to stand until needed. Sieve the flour and salt together, then add the suet and enough water to mix to a firm dough. Roll out to a 10 in (25cm) rough square about ¼ in (5mm) thick. Spread the chopped peaches and brown sugar evenly over the dough, and roll up as for a Swiss roll. Cut into 1 in (2.5cm) slices, and lay in a greased 2 pint (1.1 litre) baking dish. Remove the rind from the syrup and pour the syrup over the suet slices in the dish. Bake for 30 minutes or longer until puffed up and golden brown. Serve with custard.

Tutti-Frutti Pudding

A light sponge pudding mixed with breadcrumbs, which is full of colourful fruit, and has a sweet syrupy topping.

 Serves 4-6

3 DESSERTSPOONS GOLDEN SYRUP	3 OZ (90G) SELF-RAISING FLOUR
4 OZ (120G) BUTTER	2 OZ (60G) BREADCRUMBS
4 OZ (120G) CASTER SUGAR	2 OZ (60G) PRUNES, STONED
FINELY GRATED RIND AND JUICE	2 OZ (60G) DRIED APRICOTS
OF 1 ORANGE	2 OZ (60G) GLACÉ CHERRIES
2 EGGS	1 OZ (30G) ANGELICA

Grease a 2 pint (1.1 litre) pudding basin and cover the bottom with the syrup. Cream together the butter and sugar until light and fluffy, then add the grated orange rind. Beat the eggs to a foam, and add them gradually to the mixture. Sift the flour, mix with the breadcrumbs, and fold lightly into the pudding mixture. Chop the prunes, apricots, cherries and angelica finely and fold in with the orange juice. Pour into the basin, cover securely and steam for 2 hours. Turn out and serve with custard or Orange Sauce (see pages 122-123).

Black Cherry Marble Pudding

This pudding is good if you want to impress your friends. It looks very pretty with cherry jam sauce drifting over the cream and chocolate marbling. Remember to keep the mixture quite stiff for successful marbling.

 Serves 4-6

6 OZ (180G) BLACK CHERRY JAM	6 OZ (180G) SELF-RAISING FLOUR
4 OZ (120G) BUTTER OR MARGARINE	1 TABLESPOON COCOA POWDER
4 OZ (120G) CASTER SUGAR	1 TABLESPOON HOT WATER
2 EGGS, BEATEN	

Grease a 2 pint (1.1 litre) pudding basin and place the jam at the bottom. Beat together the butter and sugar until light and fluffy, then add the beaten egg a little at a time. Sift the flour and add to the mixture. Remove a third of the batter and add to this the cocoa and water mixed together. Place a heaped tablespoon of each of the coloured batters at alternative sides of the basin, and use all the batter up in this way. To help achieve the marble effect, a couple of gentle twists with the handle of a metal spoon helps, but don't overdo it. Cover securely, then steam for 1½-2 hours. Turn out carefully and serve with Chocolate Sauce (see pages 124-125) or custard.

Chocolate Pudding with Fudgenut Chocolate Topping

This is sheer indulgence for chocolate lovers, a moist dark chocolate sponge topped with its own delicious sauce.

 Serves 4-6

4 OZ (120G) BUTTER OR MARGARINE	3 OZ (90G) SELF-RAISING FLOUR
4 OZ (120G) SOFT BROWN SUGAR	2 HEAPED TABLESPOONS COCOA POWDER
2 EGGS, BEATEN	

Fudgenut chocolate topping

6 OZ (180G) PLAIN CHOCOLATE, BROKEN INTO PIECES	5 TABLESPOONS SINGLE CREAM
1 TABLESPOON CASTER SUGAR	2 OZ (60G) MIXED NUTS, TOASTED AND CHOPPED

Prepare the topping first by melting the chocolate in a basin standing in a saucepan of boiling water. Remove from the heat and stir in the sugar, cream and nuts. Place in the base of a buttered 3 pint (1.7 litre) pudding basin. Prepare the sponge by beating the butter or margarine and sugar together in a mixing bowl until white and fluffy. Add the eggs gradually to the creamed mixture, beating all the time. Sieve the flour and cocoa powder together and add to the mixture, stirring carefully. Turn the sponge mixture into the basin. Cover securely, and steam for 1½ hours. Turn on to a warmed plate, and serve with custard or cream.

Upside-down Winter Fruit Pudding

A basic steamed sponge cleverly decorated all over with preserved fruits of different shapes and colours. Be sure to add the greaseproof paper at the base to prevent sticking.

 Serves 4-6

Sponge

4 OZ (120G) MARGARINE	6 OZ (180G) SELF-RAISING FLOUR
4 OZ (120G) CASTER SUGAR	2 TABLESPOONS MILK
2 EGGS, BEATEN	

Fruit

2 TABLESPOONS SULTANAS	5 GLACÉ CHERRIES, HALVED
8 DATES, HALVED	4 DRIED PRUNES, HALVED
10 DRIED APRICOTS, HALVED	8 SPLIT ALMONDS

Grease a 2 pint (1.1 litre) pudding basin. Cream the margarine and caster sugar until light and fluffy, then add the beaten eggs and mix well together. Sift in the flour and stir in the milk. Put the sultanas in the base of the pudding basin. Arrange the dates in a circle up the sides around the sultanas. Pour in enough mixture to keep the dates in position. Then arrange a band of halved apricots with half a cherry inside each one around the sides of the basin above the dates, and fill the basin with more mixture. Arrange the halved prunes with a split almond replacing the stone above the apricots, and top with the remaining sponge mixture. Cover securely and steam for 2 hours. Turn out and serve with custard or Lemon Sauce (see page 122).

Dark Chocolate Pudding

This rich chocolate pudding makes a wonderful fudge sauce under the chocolate sponge topping.

 Serves 4-6

2 OZ (60G) PLAIN CHOCOLATE, CHOPPED	A PINCH OF SALT
1½ OZ (45G) BUTTER	2 OZ (60G) DARK SOFT BROWN SUGAR
¼ PINT (150ML) MILK	3 OZ (90G) CASTER SUGAR
6 OZ (180G) SUGAR	2 TABLESPOONS COCOA POWDER
4 OZ (120G) PLAIN FLOUR	7 FL OZ (200ML) WATER
2 TEASPOONS BAKING POWDER	

Preheat the oven to 160°C/325°F/Gas 3.

Put the chocolate, butter and milk into a pan and heat slowly to melt. Stir together the sugar, flour, baking powder and salt, and mix into the melted chocolate. Pour into a greased 1½ pint (900ml) baking dish. Scatter the brown sugar, caster sugar and cocoa over the top – do not mix them together – then pour on the water. Bake for 1 hour until firm. Leave to stand at room temperature until cool. Serve with its own sauce.

CHAPTER FIVE

Puddings of The Evening

THE ONLY requirement of someone attending The Pudding Club (apart from reserving a place and paying for the meal) is to bring a good appetite and happy heart. Appetite is stimulated by an aperitif served while everyone assembles, and also by the Club's unique atmosphere, once described as 'a conspiracy of naughtiness'. This atmosphere is intensified by the Host announcing, to a cascade of cheers, the names of the seven puddings to come. Then the guests are invited to take their places at tables of ten to twelve, an arrangement that encourages conviviality (and also provides the support one may need later in the evening to try just one more pudding!).

No starter is offered, to allow room for the glories to come. After the main course, expectancy mounts as the climax of the evening, the parade of puddings, is awaited. The Host will explain the Club's rule that no-one may have more than one sort of pudding in their bowl at a time; this actually adds to the party atmosphere, as everyone has to make several trips to the buffet table.

The puddings are then announced one by one, and paraded around the tables to vociferous acclaim. The assembled pudding-lovers can now go to it with a will, but there is no hurry because it is a boast of the Club that it never runs out of puddings and that no meeting ends until everyone has had their fill. So there is time to contrast and compare, to savour and reminisce, before coffee is served and the Host conducts the final ceremony, the voting (amidst the noisy and rival claims of each pudding's advocates) to establish which of the puddings has merited the honour of being 'The Pudding of the Evening'.

Here is a selection of the puddings that have most often won this accolade.

Lord Randall's Pudding

The famous ballad recording Lord Randall's caddish behaviour, and his ensuing death at the hands of one of his family, seems to have no connection with this pudding. Pudding Club members would doubt that such a rotter could be a pudding lover.

 Serves 4-6

5 OZ (150G) PLAIN FLOUR	6 FL OZ (175ML) MILK
I TEASPOON BICARBONATE OF SODA	5 OZ (150G) DRIED APRICOTS,
5 OZ (150G) BUTTER	CHOPPED
4 OZ (120G) SOFT BROWN SUGAR	5 OZ (150G) THICK DARK
I EGG, BEATEN	MARMALADE

Sift the flour and bicarbonate of soda together. Cream the butter and sugar together until light and fluffy. Add the beaten egg, milk, flour and apricots separately to the butter mixture. Beat vigorously and then finally stir in the marmalade. Turn the mixture into a greased 2 pint (1.1 litre) pudding basin and cover securely. Steam for 1½-2 hours. Turn out and serve with custard.

Apricot Queen of Puddings

This is The Pudding Club's de-luxe version of the old classic. A delicious light pudding is topped with a golden brown crusty meringue.

 Serves 4-6

6 OZ (180G) BREADCRUMBS	½ TEASPOON VANILLA ESSENCE
1 OZ (30G) CASTER SUGAR	4 EGG YOLKS
FINELY GRATED RIND OF 1 LEMON	1 LB (480G) TINNED APRICOTS OR
1 PINT (600ML) MILK	FRESH APRICOTS, STEWED
2 OZ (60G) BUTTER	

Meringue

4 EGG WHITES	4 OZ (120G) CASTER SUGAR

Preheat the oven to 180°C/350°F/Gas 4.

Put the breadcrumbs, sugar and lemon rind in a mixing bowl. Warm the milk, butter and vanilla essence until the butter is melted and then pour over the crumbs. Leave the mixture to stand for 10 minutes then beat in the egg yolks.

Grease a 2 pint (1.1 litre) pie dish and pour in the mixture. Bake for 20-30 minutes until well set.

Drain the apricots and arrange in slices over the pudding. Whisk the egg whites until stiff. Fold in the sugar and spread over the apricots. Place the pudding back in the oven for about 10 minutes until the meringue is lightly browned and crisp.

Queen of Puddings

As previous page, but spread the pudding generously with jam instead of topping with apricots. The jam may need to be warmed to enable it to spread easily.

Syrup Sponge

No pudding engenders more rivalry between members of The Pudding Club, or more return visits for seconds, than this sponge pudding soaked with syrup.

Serves 4-6

4 OZ (120G) BUTTER	2 EGGS, BEATEN
4 OZ (120G) CASTER SUGAR	2 TABLESPOONS GOLDEN SYRUP
4 OZ (120G) SELF-RAISING FLOUR	

Cream the butter and sugar together until light and fluffy. Sift the flour and add this to the creamed mixture along with the egg, a little at a time, beating well. Put the golden syrup in the base of a buttered 2 pint (1.1 litre) pudding basin, and pour the sponge mixture carefully over the syrup. Cover securely and steam for 1½-2 hours. Turn out and serve with Syrup Sauce (see page 122) and custard.

Tip

Always rinse the tablespoon in hot water and warm the syrup slightly by standing the open can in hot water. This makes the syrup easier to get off the spoon.

Apricot Queen of Puddings is The Pudding Club's
de-luxe version of the popular classic.
See page 95.

 Apples and sultanas are layered with thin circles of suet pastry,
then steamed for Spicy Apple Layer Pudding.
See page 107

Made with pineapple and glacé cherries, the spectacular
Holiday Pudding is served with its own fruity sauce.
See page 110.

Ground almonds replace the flour in the unusual topping
for Apricot and Almond Crumble.
See page 113.

Lemon Sponge

Make the Syrup Sponge mixture as before, adding the finely grated rind and juice of 1 lemon to the mixture, and spreading the base of the pudding dish with 2 tablespoons lemon curd instead of the syrup. Steam as before, turn out and serve with Lemon Sauce (see page 122) and custard.

Jam and Coconut Sponge

This pudding uses the same Syrup Sponge mixture with the syrup replaced by 2 tablespoons dark red jam spread in the bottom of the basin. Add 2 oz (60g) desiccated coconut to the sponge mixture. Steam as before, turn out and serve with custard. If you can get it, damson jam gives the best results, because its dark colour contrasts with the pale coconut.

Winter Lemon Pudding

This is a good pudding for a blustery wet day. The lemon and butter filling will not necessarily cure a cold, but will make you feel better about life in general.

 Serves 6

Suet pastry

8 OZ (240G) SELF-RAISING FLOUR	4 OZ (120G) SHREDDED SUET
A PINCH OF SALT	WATER TO MIX

Filling

2 EGGS	FINELY GRATED RIND AND JUICE
6 OZ (180G) SUGAR	OF 2 LEMONS
	2 OZ (60G) BUTTER, MELTED

Sift the flour and salt together and then mix with the suet. Add enough cold water to make a soft dough. Roll half the pastry out, and use to line a greased 2 pint (1.1 litre) pudding basin. Divide the rest of the pastry roughly into two, and roll these pieces out to make graduated layers of pastry for the middle and top of the pudding.

For the filling, beat together the eggs, sugar, lemon rind, juice, and melted butter. Pour half of this mixture into the lined basin, add the centre layer of pastry, pour in the remaining mixture and top with the final layer of pastry. Cover securely and steam for 2½-3 hours. Turn out and serve with lashings of custard.

Sticky Toffee Pudding

This pudding has always been a top favourite with Pudding Club members. It can be made in advance, kept in a refrigerator and reheated.

 ## Serves 8

4 OZ (120G) BUTTER, SOFTENED	8 OZ (240G) STONED DATES,
6 OZ (180G) SOFT BROWN SUGAR	CHOPPED
4 EGGS, BEATEN	2 TEASPOONS CAMP COFFEE
8 OZ (240G) SELF-RAISING FLOUR	½ PINT (300ML) BOILING WATER
I TEASPOON BICARBONATE OF SODA	

Preheat the oven to 180°C/350°F/Gas 4.

Cream the butter and sugar together thoroughly. Add the beaten egg a little at a time. If it starts to curdle, add some of the flour. Sieve the flour and bicarbonate of soda together, and fold into the creamed mixture. Add the dates, coffee and hot water, and mix thoroughly, it should be a very soft batter. Pour into an 8 in (20cm) non-stick cake tin. Bake for about 1½ hours. Turn out and serve with Butterscotch Sauce (see page 123).

Spotted Dick

The name of this pudding always raises a laugh in Britain, but gets horrified gasps from our American friends, who blush at something that to them is shockingly explicit. However, if decorum is needed at the dinner table, the pudding can also be called Spotted Dog . . .

 Serves 4-6

8 OZ (240G) SELF-RAISING FLOUR	8 OZ (240G) CURRANTS OR
A PINCH OF SALT	RAISINS, SOAKED IN BRANDY
4 OZ (120G) SHREDDED SUET	¼ PINT (150ML) COLD WATER
1 OZ (30G) SUGAR	

Grease a 2 pint (1.1 litre) pudding basin. Sieve together the flour and salt, then add the shredded suet, sugar and dried fruit. Mix these ingredients with enough water to make a firm dough. Cover securely and steam for 2 hours. Turn the pudding out on to a hot dish and serve with custard.

 Tip

If you want to make a spotted dick in the traditional shape, form the mixture into a cylinder of about 8 in (20cm) long, and roll in a pudding cloth (see page 18). Boil for 2 hours.

Coffee and Walnut Pudding

This is a simple baked pudding, but the blend of coffee and walnuts with sultanas is magical, and it is particularly good served with custard or warmed golden syrup.

 Serves 4-6

4 OZ (120G) BUTTER	4 OZ (120G) SELF-RAISING FLOUR
5 OZ (150G) MUSCOVADO SUGAR	2 TABLESPOONS MILK
1 EGG, BEATEN	1 TABLESPOON VEGETABLE OIL
2 TABLESPOONS INSTANT COFFEE DISSOLVED IN 2 TABLESPOONS HOT WATER	2 OZ (60G) SHELLED WALNUTS, CHOPPED
	2 OZ (60G) SULTANAS

Preheat the oven to 160°C/325°F/Gas 3.

Beat the butter and sugar together until light and fluffy, then beat in the egg and coffee mixture. Sift the flour, and add it gradually to the mixture, then add the milk and oil to form a dropping consistency. Add the nuts and sultanas, and mix well. Spoon into a greased 2 pint (1.1 litre) baking dish and bake for 50 minutes.

Very Chocolate Pudding

Chocolate chips are added to the basin to give this pudding a soft chocolate topping, and to make its chocolate content even greater.

 Serves 4-6

4 OZ (120G) BUTTER	1 OZ (30G) COCOA POWDER
4 OZ (120G) CASTER SUGAR	2 EGGS
4 OZ (120G) SELF-RAISING FLOUR	2 OZ (60G) CHOCOLATE CHIPS

Cream the butter and sugar together until light and fluffy. Sift the flour and cocoa together and add with the egg, a little at a time, to the creamed mixture, beating well between each addition. Finally, stir in half the chocolate chips. Place a covering of the remaining chocolate chips over the base of a greased 2 pint (1.1 litre) pudding basin before adding the mixture. Steam for 1½-2 hours. Turn out and serve with, inevitably, Chocolate Sauce (see pages 124-5).

Victoria's Pudding

This is The Pudding Club's recipe for Victoria's Pudding. Mr Francatelli gave a recipe for Victoria's Pudding in his *Modern Cookery* in 1862, and it appeared on banquet menus while he was Royal Chef.

 Serves 6-8

2 OZ (60G) STONED DATES, CHOPPED	½ CUP COLD TEA
2 OZ (60G) DEMERARA SUGAR	3 OZ (90G) WHOLEMEAL SELF-RAISING FLOUR
1 OZ (30G) GLACÉ CHERRIES, CHOPPED	2 OZ (60G) WHOLEMEAL BREADCRUMBS
6 OZ (180G) RAISINS	2 TABLESPOONS SUNFLOWER OIL
1 PINCH OF GROUND NUTMEG	1 SMALL BANANA, PEELED AND MASHED
¼ TEASPOON MIXED SPICE	
2 TEASPOONS HONEY	1 EGG, BEATEN
2 TEASPOONS RUM	

Mix the first nine ingredients together in a large bowl. Cover and leave for a few hours or overnight.

Mix the remaining ingredients together, and then mix into the first bowl until well incorporated. Transfer to a greased 3 pint (1.7 litre) pudding basin, cover securely and steam for 5½ hours, adding more boiling water as necessary. This pudding keeps very well, requiring 1½ hours' steaming to reheat.

Bread and Butter Pudding

This pudding has enjoyed a renaissance recently, mainly through the recipes of some of our leading chefs, and has been somewhat elevated from its humble origins. Pudding Club version uses white bread and some simple flavourings, and is a constant winner at PC evenings.

 Serves 4-6

10-12 SLICES WHITE BREAD, WITHOUT CRUSTS	3 EGGS
4-6 OZ (120-180G) BUTTER, SOFTENED	1 PINT (600ML) MILK
JUICE AND FINELY GRATED RIND OF 1 ORANGE	3 OZ (90G) CASTER SUGAR
4 OZ (120G) SULTANAS, SOAKED IN BRANDY	POWDERED CINNAMON OR GROUND NUTMEG

Preheat the oven to 200°C/400°F/Gas 6.

Grease a 2 pint (1.1 litre) ovenproof baking dish. Butter the bread. Line the bottom and sides of the dish with some of the bread and sprinkle with the orange juice and rind. Add half the sultanas, followed by another layer of bread, the remaining sultanas and finally the remaining bread. Beat the eggs well, add the milk and sugar, and pour this mixture over the bread. Sprinkle with cinnamon or nutmeg, and bake for 30 minutes or until set. Serve hot on its own, or with custard.

 Tip

Do not let any sultanas sit on top of the pudding while it is cooking as they will become hard and taste burnt.

The pudding is improved if allowed to soak for half an hour before putting it in the oven.

Jam Roly-Poly

One of the great all-time favourites at The Pudding Club (sometimes called Rowley-Powley in old recipe books). It can be steamed in a cloth – the traditional way – or baked in the oven.

 Serves 4-6

6 OZ (180G) SELF-RAISING FLOUR	½ OZ (15G) SUGAR
A PINCH OF SALT	1 LB (480G) GOOD-QUALITY DARK
3 OZ (90G) SHREDDED SUET	RED JAM
WATER TO MIX	

Preheat the oven to 190-200°C/375-400°F/Gas 5-6.

Sift the flour and salt together, then add the suet and enough water to make a good rolling dough. Roll the dough out to approximately 10 in (25cm) square. Spread the dough with a thick layer of jam. Dampen the edges with water to seal, and roll up like a Swiss roll. Place in a roasting tin (see our tip), and bake for about 1 hour. Turn the pudding out of the tin carefully and roll gently on to a serving dish. Serve with custard.

 Tip

To prevent the roly-poly flattening out, place it in a roasting tin, and tip the tin up so the roly-poly rolls into one end, which helps to keep the roly-poly shape.

Apple and Almond Pudding

This delicious pudding uses a sweet batter enclosing a combination of apples and almonds.

 Serves 4-6

6 OZ (180G) SELF-RAISING FLOUR	8 OZ (240G) COOKING APPLES,
½ TEASPOON BAKING POWDER	WEIGHED AFTER PEELING AND
4 OZ (120G) MARGARINE, MELTED	CORING
6 OZ (180G) CASTER SUGAR	I OZ (30G) FLAKED ALMONDS
2 EGGS, BEATEN	A SPRINKLING OF DEMERARA SUGAR
I½ TEASPOONS ALMOND ESSENCE	

Preheat the oven to 160°C/325°F/Gas 3.

Sift the flour and baking powder together, and place with the rest of the ingredients, except the apples, almonds and demerara sugar, into a mixing bowl. Mix well until smooth. Spread half the mixture over the bottom of a greased 2 pint (1.1 litre) baking dish. Cover with the prepared apples and then dot with spoonfuls of the remaining mixture. Sprinkle with almonds and demerara sugar. Bake for about 1¼ hours until pale gold and shrinking away from the sides of the tin. Serve with custard.

Spicy Apple Layer Pudding

Another version of this goes under the rather grand name of De La Ware pudding (sometimes Brigade Pudding); this is made from half apple and half mincemeat (a good way of using up mincemeat after Christmas). Yet another version uses apricots and mincemeat.

 ## Serves 4-6

Suet pastry

8 OZ (240G) SELF-RAISING FLOUR	4 OZ (120G) SHREDDED SUET
A PINCH OF SALT	¼ PINT (150ML) WATER

Filling

2 TABLESPOONS GOLDEN SYRUP	5 OZ (150G) DEMERARA SUGAR
4 LARGE COOKING APPLES, CORED,	4 OZ (120G) SULTANAS
PEELED AND SLICED	I TEASPOON POWDERED CINNAMON
2 TABLESPOONS LEMON JUICE	

To make the suet pastry, sift the flour and salt into a mixing bowl, add the suet and water and mix to a stiff dough. Divide roughly into four pieces and press or roll out into graduated circles to fit a greased 2 pint (1.1 litre) pudding basin. Place the syrup in the bottom of the basin. Mix the remaining filling ingredients together. Alternate the pastry and the filling, starting with pastry and finishing off with a pastry top. Cover securely and steam for 2½-3 hours. Turn out on to a serving dish, and serve with custard.

Syrup Layer Pudding

This pudding uses the same suet pastry and method as the Spicy Apple Layer Pudding, but with this syrup, breadcrumb and lemon filling.

5 TABLESPOONS GOLDEN SYRUP, WARMED	8 OZ (240G) WHITE BREADCRUMBS
	1 TABLESPOON LEMON JUICE

Mix these filling ingredients together, spread between layers of suet pastry as before, and steam as before.

Granny's Irish Pudding

This is a big pudding, and benefits from standing for a few hours before steaming. It can also be cooked as a cannonball pudding in a cloth.

Serves up to 12

6 OZ (180G) SELF-RAISING FLOUR	1 TABLESPOON THICK MARMALADE
A PINCH OF SALT	1 TEASPOON GROUND GINGER
4 OZ (120G) SHREDDED SUET	1½ TEASPOONS MIXED SPICE
4 OZ (120G) SUGAR	1 EGG, BEATEN
2 OZ (60G) BREADCRUMBS	1 TABLESPOON RUM
6 OZ (180G) MIXED DRIED FRUIT	1 BOTTLE GUINNESS
2 OZ (60G) GLACÉ CHERRIES, CHOPPED	

Sift the flour and salt together, and then mix in all the remaining ingredients except for the Guinness. Add enough of this to bring the mixture to a dropping consistency. Grease a 4 pint (2.3 litre) pudding basin, transfer the mixture to it, and cover securely. Steam for 3 hours. Turn out and serve hot with custard. Leftover slices can be dusted with cinnamon and fried in butter.

Chocolate and Walnut Fudge Pudding

This pudding's win at a Pudding Club evening resulted in a two-page spread in one of the Sunday colour supplements, and put The Pudding Club firmly on the map.

 Serves 4-6

3 OZ (90G) MARGARINE	I OZ (30G) COCOA POWDER
3 OZ (90G) SUGAR	2 EGGS, BEATEN
3 OZ (90G) SELF-RAISING FLOUR	

Topping

I OZ (30G) COCOA POWDER	2 OZ (60G) SHELLED WALNUTS,
½ PINT (300ML) BLACK COFFEE	CHOPPED
4 OZ (120G) DEMERARA SUGAR	

Preheat the oven to 180°C/350°F/Gas 4.

Cream the margarine and sugar together. Sift the flour and cocoa together, then add the beaten eggs to the first mixture, along with the flour mixture, and beat well. Spoon into a greased 2 pint (1.1 litre) baking dish. For the topping, blend the cocoa into the black coffee, add the sugar and walnuts, and pour over the pudding mixture. Bake for approximately 45 minutes. Serve with custard or cream.

Holiday Pudding

Serves 4-6

2 TABLESPOONS GOLDEN SYRUP	3 OZ (90G) SELF-RAISING FLOUR
1 X 8 OZ (225G) TIN PINEAPPLE	A PINCH OF SALT
RINGS	2 OZ (60G) BREADCRUMBS
2 OZ (60G) GLACÉ CHERRIES	2 OZ (60G) RAISINS
4 OZ (120G) SOFT MARGARINE	1 OZ (30G) CANDIED PEEL
4 OZ (120G) CASTER SUGAR	1 OZ (30G) SHELLED WALNUTS,
2 LARGE EGGS, BEATEN	CHOPPED

Sauce

JUICE FROM THE PINEAPPLE TIN	6 FL OZ (175ML) WHITE WINE
JUICE OF 1 LEMON AND 1 ORANGE	1 TABLESPOON CORNFLOUR
6 FL OZ (175ML) WATER	SUGAR TO TASTE

Grease a 2½ pint (1.4 litre) pudding basin, and line the base with a circle of greaseproof paper. Put the golden syrup into the basin, and arrange 1 drained pineapple ring in the bottom with a cherry in the centre. Cut 2 rings in half and arrange these halves around the first ring. Put a cherry in the centre of each. Drain (reserving the juices) and chop the remaining pineapple rings; chop the remaining glacé cherries. Cream the margarine and sugar together then add the beaten eggs. Sift the flour and salt, then add with the breadcrumbs. Mix well then stir in all the fruit, peel and nuts. Pile the mixture on top of the arranged fruit. Cover securely and steam for 1½ hours before turning out.

Meanwhile, for the sauce, mix the liquids together in a small pan. Mix a little of this with the cornflour, then add to the pan. Add sugar to taste and heat gently, stirring all the time, until the sauce thickens. Pour over the pudding.

CHAPTER SIX

Crumbles
and Other
Toppings

E VERYONE LOVES fruit puddings, and although we have a
chapter devoted to traditional seasonal fruit puddings, here
we have gathered together some of the simple toppings that can
transform fruit, raw, stewed or tinned. To stew fruit, cook over a
gentle heat with a little water and sugar to taste. Remove stones if
necessary and skins if desired. Then top with crumble, flapjack, suet
pastry or sponge and bake until golden.

Some fruits are especially good in particular combinations.
The following are highly recommended:

rhubarb and ginger (chopped stem or ground)
blackcurrant and rhubarb
strawberry and gooseberry
raspberry and redcurrant
blackberry and apple.

The first recipe uses the simplest of all toppings – breadcrumbs and suet alone.

Quick Apple Pudding

This is a really basic recipe. Try it with apples and then devise your own variations – plums, gooseberries or blackberries would be equally good.

8 OZ (240G) BREADCRUMBS	SUGAR TO TASTE
3 OZ (90G) SHREDDED SUET	2-3 WHOLE CLOVES
1 LB (480G) COOKING APPLES, PEELED, CORED AND SLICED	

Preheat the oven to 180°C/350°F/Gas 4.

Mix the breadcrumbs and suet together. Grease a 2 pint (1.1 litre) pie dish and put in a layer of sliced apple with sugar to taste and cloves, followed by a layer of crumb mixture. Repeat these layers until the dish is full, topping with crumbs and suet. Bake for 25-30 minutes. Serve with custard or cream.

Crumble Mix

Crumble mix is very versatile. Porridge oats can be added or a little desiccated coconut. Dark brown sugar can be used instead of granulated.

 Serves 4-6

3 OZ (90G) MARGARINE	3 OZ (90G) SUGAR
6 OZ (180G) SELF-RAISING FLOUR	

Preheat the oven to 180°C/350°F/Gas 4.

Rub the margarine into the flour until it resembles breadcrumbs, then mix in the sugar. Spoon the mixture over the chosen fruit and bake in the oven for about 30 minutes until golden.

Apricot and Almond Crumble

This is a particularly good variation on the basic recipe. The almonds help give a good nutty flavour and texture. Tinned apricots are good, but always use fresh when they are in the shops.

 ## Serves 4-6

12 APRICOTS	12 BLANCHED ALMONDS
CASTER SUGAR TO TASTE	

Crumble topping

3 OZ (90G) BUTTER	2 OZ (60G) CASTER SUGAR
4 OZ (120G) PLAIN FLOUR	2 OZ (60G) GROUND ALMONDS

Preheat the oven to 180°C/350°F/Gas 4.

Quarter the apricots and arrange in a greased shallow 10 in (25cm) baking dish. Sprinkle with extra sugar to taste, if using fresh apricots. Rub the butter into the flour until it resembles fine crumbs, and mix in the caster sugar and the ground almonds. Spread over the fruit and top with the blanched almonds. Bake for about 30 minutes or until golden brown. Serve with custard or cream.

Flapjack Mix

This has to be made as it is needed, but again it is quick and easy.

 Serves 4-6

3 OZ (90G) MARGARINE	I TABLESPOON GOLDEN SYRUP
3 OZ (90G) SOFT BROWN SUGAR	4 OZ (120G) PORRIDGE OATS

Preheat the oven to 180°C/350°F/Gas 4.

Melt the margarine, sugar and syrup together and then stir in the oats. Spread this mixture over the chosen fruit and bake for 30 minutes until brown and crisp on top. Serve all fruit flapjacks with custard.

Blackcurrant Flapjack

 This is especially popular at The Pudding Club. We use fresh berries when in season, but frozen ones are just as good and are easier to spread the flapjack mixture over. The tartness of the fruit is excellent with the sweet flapjack.

Rhubarb Flapjack

 This is also popular, because of rhubarb's tartness. Here ground ginger can be scattered on the rhubarb or chopped stem ginger added with some of the syrup.

Apple Flapjack

This is a flapjack with a difference. Instead of covering the fruit, a crunchy syrupy envelope of flapjack surrounds an apple filling. This pudding is good with other fruits – try rhubarb or stoned plums. Save a few slices of apples to decorate the top of the pudding.

 Serves 4-6

2 LB (960G) COOKING APPLES, PEELED, CORED AND SLICED	4 TABLESPOONS GOLDEN SYRUP
2½ OZ (75G) SUGAR	8 OZ (240G) ROLLED OATS
5 OZ (150G) BUTTER	¼ TEASPOON SALT
	I TEASPOON GROUND GINGER

To decorate

ICING SUGAR	BUTTER
A FEW APPLE SLICES FROM ABOVE	SUGAR

Preheat the oven to 190°C/375°F/Gas 5.

Simmer most of the apple gently with 1½ oz (45g) of the sugar in a covered pan, until soft and pulpy. Grease a shallow 8 in (20cm) pie dish. Heat the remaining sugar, butter and syrup together gently until dissolved. Stir in the oats, salt and ground ginger.

Line the base and sides of the dish to within 1 in (2.5cm) of the top using three-quarters of the oat mixture. Pour the apples into the centre and cover with the remaining oat mixture. Press down lightly. Then bake for about 35 minutes. Dredge with icing sugar and decorate with apple slices gently fried in butter with a little sugar. Serve with custard.

Suet Pastry Topping

A suet pastry is filling and tasty, and goes a crisp golden-brown when baked, which is most appetising. The fruit underneath must be hot.

 Serves 4-6

6 OZ (180G) SELF–RAISING FLOUR	MILK OR WATER TO MIX
3 OZ (90G) SHREDDED SUET	

Preheat the oven to 180°C/350°F/Gas 4.

Put the flour and suet in a bowl, and mix to a dough with the liquid. A stiff dough can be patted out on a floured board to roughly the required shape and placed over hot fruit in a pie dish, or a softer dough can be spooned on to the hot fruit like dumplings. In both cases, cook for 30 minutes.

Toffee Apple Pudding

This is a fancier version of the above. The suet crust is baked golden brown with the apples caramelising inside.

 Serves 4-6

6 OZ (180G) SELF-RAISING FLOUR	1 TABLESPOON LEMON JUICE
A PINCH OF SALT	4 OZ (120G) DEMERARA SUGAR
3 OZ (90G) SHREDDED SUET	1 TABLESPOON GOLDEN SYRUP
COLD WATER TO MIX	
4 COOKING APPLES, PEELED, CORED AND SLICED	

Preheat the oven to 180°C/350°F/Gas 4.

Sift the flour and salt together, and mix in the suet. Add enough water to make a fairly stiff dough. Use half of this mixture to line a greased 2 pint (1.1 litre) pie dish. Add the chopped apple, lemon juice and half the sugar and cover with the rest of the dough. Moisten edges and press well to seal. Bake for 20 minutes, then remove from the oven, spread with syrup and sprinkle with the remaining sugar. Place back in the oven and bake until golden brown, another 20 minutes or so. Serve with custard.

Rhubarb and Plum Whirligig

Another way of using a suet pastry as a topping, as crunchy whirls (see Apple Dappy too, page 52).

 Serves 4-6

I LB (480G) FRESH RHUBARB	3 OZ (90G) SHREDDED SUET
I LB (480G) FRESH OR TINNED RED PLUMS	2 OZ (60G) CASTER SUGAR
½ TEASPOON GROUND GINGER	WATER TO MIX
6 OZ (180G) SELF-RAISING FLOUR	ABOUT 3 TABLESPOONS MARMALADE
	A LITTLE DEMERARA SUGAR

Preheat the oven to 190°C/375°F/Gas 5.

Clean and roughly chop the rhubarb. Cut the plums in half and remove the stones. If using fresh plums, stew gently with a little extra sugar to taste until soft enough to remove the stones easily. Place the rhubarb, plums and ginger into a 10 in (25cm) ovenproof dish. Make sure the dish is deep enough to contain the hot juice created by the cooked rhubarb. Mix the flour, suet and sugar in a large bowl. Add enough water to make a firm dough. Roll out on a floured board to approximately 10 in (25cm) square and spread the marmalade over. Roll up like a Swiss roll and cut into 8 or 10 slices. Arrange these over the fruit, and sprinkle with a little demerara sugar. Bake for 30-40 minutes or until the whirls are risen and golden. Serve warm with custard, cream or ice cream.

Simple Sponge Topping

As this is a Victoria sponge mix, you could double it and bake a sponge cake (for tea next day or a trifle) at the same time as your pud. The fruit underneath the sponge topping should be hot.

 Serves 4-6

2 OZ (60G) MARGARINE	1 EGG, BEATEN
2 OZ (60G) CASTER SUGAR	2 OZ (60G) SELF-RAISING FLOUR

Preheat the oven to 180°C/350°F/Gas 4.

Cream the margarine and sugar together until light and fluffy. Beat in the egg with a little flour, then fold in the rest of the flour. Spoon the mixture over your chosen hot fruit, and bake for 30 minutes.

Fluffy Apple and Almond Pudding

This especially delicious version uses almonds instead of flour in the sponge topping.

 Serves 4-6

4 COOKING APPLES, PEELED, CORED AND CHOPPED	3 OZ (90G) BUTTER
2 OZ (60G) BREADCRUMBS, TOASTED	2 OZ (60G) GROUND ALMONDS
	A FEW DROPS OF ALMOND ESSENCE
2 OZ (60G) CASTER SUGAR	6 EGGS, BEATEN
	A FEW BLANCHED ALMONDS

Preheat the oven to 180°C/350°F/Gas 4.

Cook the apples slowly in a spoonful or so of water until soft. Mix them with the crumbs and put into a greased 2 pint (1.1 litre) pie dish. Then mix together the sugar, butter, ground almonds, almond essence and the beaten eggs. Spread this mixture on top of the apples and crumbs. Decorate with split blanched almonds, and bake for 45 minutes. Serve with custard or cream.

Tip

To toast crumbs, spread them over a piece of foil, and toast – carefully – under the grill. Turn them over to brown all sides.

CHAPTER SEVEN

Apart from Custard

CUSTARD IS the perfect accompaniment to most puddings and especially to all hot puddings, but the following sauces are recommended, not necessarily to the exclusion of custard.

Brandy (or Rum) Butter

Brandy butter, sometimes known as hard sauce, is the traditional accompaniment to Christmas pudding, but is also very good with fruit puddings. It can be made in advance and kept in the refrigerator.

4 OZ (120G) UNSALTED BUTTER, SOFTENED	3–4 TABLESPOONS BRANDY (OR RUM)
4 OZ (120G) CASTER SUGAR	

Beat the butter and sugar together until pale, smooth and creamy. Add the brandy (or rum) a tablespoon at a time, beating the mixture well after each addition. Place the finished butter in a jar and chill until needed.

Syrup Sauce

Serve with Syrup Sponge (see page 96), or a variety of other puds.

1 DESSERTSPOON CORNFLOUR	2 TABLESPOONS GOLDEN SYRUP
5 FL OZ (150ML) WATER	JUICE OF ½ LEMON

Mix the cornflour with a little of the water, then add all the other ingredients. Heat in a small pan, stirring all the time, until the sauce thickens. Serve hot.

Creamy Toffee Sauce

Good with Spotted Dick and some of the plainer fruit puds.

6 FL OZ (175ML) DOUBLE CREAM	2 OZ (60G) BUTTER
2 OZ (60G) BROWN SUGAR	

Place the ingredients in a small saucepan, and heat through very gently. Do not let the mixture boil. When hot pour into a sauceboat.

Lemon (or Orange) Sauce

A sharp fruity sauce is sometimes needed to counteract the sweetness of puddings. This sauce will also liven up a plain pudding

1½ TABLESPOONS CORNFLOUR	JUICE AND FINELY GRATED RIND
¾ PINT (450ML) WATER	OF 1 LEMON (OR ORANGE)
2 OZ (60G) SUGAR	

Mix the cornflour with a little of the water, and place all the ingredients in a saucepan. Gently bring to the boil and cook for 2 minutes, stirring constantly until it thickens a little. Serve hot.

Orange Sauce

A luxurious orange sauce, particularly good with the Orange and Coconut Pudding on page 123.

1 TEASPOON CORNFLOUR	1 FL OZ (30ML) COINTREAU OR
4 FL OZ (125ML) FRESH ORANGE	BRANDY
JUICE	JUICE OF ½ LEMON

Mix the cornflour with the orange juice, add the remaining ingredients and heat gently until boiling. Boil for 3 minutes until the mixture becomes clear and thickens. Serve hot.

Butterscotch Sauce

An essential accompaniment for many puddings, especially Sticky Toffee and Gingerbread on pages 99 and 31.

2 OZ (60G) BUTTER	1 TABLESPOON GOLDEN SYRUP
5 OZ (150G) DEMERARA SUGAR	5 OZ (150G) EVAPORATED MILK

Melt the butter, then add the sugar and syrup and stir until dissolved. Pour in the milk, turn up the heat, and beat until boiling. Serve hot.

Ginger Sauce

Try this ginger sauce with ginger-flavoured puddings, or fruit puddings for a change.

1 TABLESPOON CORNFLOUR	4 TABLESPOONS DRAINED AND
8 FL OZ (250ML) WATER	PRESERVED GINGER, CHOPPED
3 OZ (90G) SOFT BROWN SUGAR	1 TABLESPOON LEMON JUICE

Mix the cornflour with a little of the water. Heat the remaining water and sugar together until the sugar is dissolved. Add the ginger and lemon juice, bring to the boil, then add the cornflour mixture and boil for 2-3 minutes until clear. Serve hot.

Creamy Chocolate Sauce

A simple sauce with cream beaten in for extra richness.

2 TABLESPOONS CORNFLOUR	¾ PINT (450ML) MILK
2 TABLESPOONS COCOA POWDER	¼ PINT (150ML) SINGLE CREAM
2 TABLESPOONS CASTER SUGAR	

Blend the cornflour, cocoa and sugar with a little of the milk. Heat the rest of the milk until almost boiling, add the blended mixture, mix well and return to the heat. Bring to the boil and cook for 1-2 minutes, stirring constantly, until the sauce thickens. Remove from the heat and beat in the single cream.

Rich Chocolate Sauce

To accompany a chocolate pudding, or as a sauce for other puddings.

6 OZ (180G) GOOD PLAIN CHOCOLATE, BROKEN INTO PIECES	6 FL OZ (175 ML) WATER
	4 OZ (120G) SUGAR
	2 OZ (60G) BUTTER

Place all the ingredients in a saucepan, and heat gently until melted. Serve hot.

Apricot Sauce

This is a good sauce recipe for plain puddings.

1 TABLESPOON CORNFLOUR	2 OZ (60G) SUGAR
6 FL OZ (175ML) WATER	6 FL OZ (175ML) WHITE WINE
2 TABLESPOONS APRICOT JAM	

Mix the cornflour with a little of the water. Heat the other ingredients in a small pan, stirring all the time. Add the cornflour as it comes to the boil, and continue to stir until you have a delicious smooth sauce. Serve hot.

Rich White Sauce

Add more flavour with a little alcohol – rum, brandy or sherry.

I TABLESPOON CORNFLOUR	I OZ (30G) SUGAR
½ PINT (300ML) MILK	I OZ (30G) BUTTER

Mix the cornflour with a little of the milk, and stir into the remaining milk. Add the sugar and butter, and slowly bring to the boil. Cook gently until the mixture thickens, then simmer slowly for 3 minutes. Serve hot.

Lemon Custard Sauce

This is particularly good with the Date and Lemon Pudding on page 35.

½ OZ (15G) CORNFLOUR	FINELY GRATED RIND AND JUICE
½ OZ (15G) CUSTARD POWDER	OF I LEMON
¾ PINT (450ML) MILK	I OZ (30G) BUTTER
I OZ (30G) SUGAR	

Mix the cornflour and custard powder with a little of the milk, then add the rest of the milk and the sugar. Heat gently in a small pan, stirring constantly until thickened, about 2-3 minutes. Stir in the rind, juice and butter when cooked.

Index